The Ladies' Loos

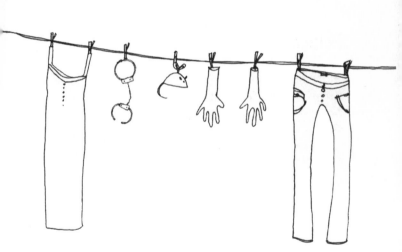

A percentage of the profit from this book will be divided between the following charities:

R▲PECRISIS
ENGLAND AND WALES

Rape Crisis (England & Wales) is the national coordinating and support agency for rape crisis centres. The charity lobbies government and other bodies to improve services for survivors of rape and sexual violence and to reduce the incidence of sexual violence. It also works in partnership with others to raise awareness of issues surrounding sexual violence towards women.
www.rapecrisis.org.uk

Refuge
For women and children.
Against domestic violence.

Refuge is the UK's largest single provider of specialist accommodation and support to women and children escaping domestic violence – a national 'lifeline' for up to 80 000 women and children every year. Refuge provides safe, emergency accommodation through a growing network of refuges throughout the UK and runs a 24 hour national domestic violence helpline, in partnership with Women's Aid.
www.refuge.org.uk

SAMARITANS

Samaritans offers confidential, non-judgemental, emotional support 24 hours a day. The charity gives millions of people the time and space to explore their feelings and options – never judging, always confidential, providing the power of active listening to support people in need, 24 hours a day, 7 days a week.
www.samaritans.org

The Ladies' Loos

From Plumbing to Plucking, a Practical Guide for Girls

Natasha Morabito & Kate Harrad

FRIDAY BOOKS

First published in Great Britain in 2006 by Friday Books
An imprint of The Friday Project Limited
83 Victoria Street, London SW1H 0H
www.thefridayproject.co.uk
www.fridaybooks.co.uk

British Library Cataloguing in Publication Data.
A catalogue record for this book is available from
the British Library.

ISBN 10 – 1 905548 30 3
ISBN 13 – 978 1 905548 30 9

Designed and produced by Staziker Jones
www.stazikerjones.co.uk
Illustrations by Lucy Daniels

The Publisher's policy is to use paper manufactured
from sustainable forests.

Contents

Introduction

What do you talk about in the Ladies' Loos with your friends? There is something very special about that space where girls gather unobserved and uninterrupted. Something that means that no subject is out of bounds.

The Ladies' Loos started out as a private online community for women, and it's from that community that all the advice in this book has been taken.

One of the strengths of the Ladies' Loos is that the membership is made up of women from practically all backgrounds and cultures, and yet (on the whole) we get on very well and try our best to give each other advice without judgement. The membership is made up of women aged from late teens to the over-50s, straight, gay, bi-, poly-, trans-, mothers, the child-free, students, professors, Goths and fashion victims (though who says you can't be both of those?).

We have members outside the UK too – particularly the USA, Germany and Greece – but plenty of others as well.

The idea of trying to make a book out of the most useful information posted on the forums stuck in my head for quite a while. I decided to ask what the others felt about it, and when I got a positive response

I contacted the people who would eventually become my publishers; I was really glad that we were working with all women at the publishing company too.

I asked the Ladies if anyone wanted to come along to our first meeting with me, and Kate Harrad quickly volunteered to lend her talent and expertise to the project. Not long afterwards she became my co-editor. She's done a lot of writing and is terribly well organised (I haven't and I'm not!), so this suited me down to the ground.

As I remember it, Kate and I met up in an old man's pub in Waterloo the day before our meeting; I drank booze and rambled, while she had a notebook (and took notes!) and stuck to apple juice.

The next question was which charities we'd like to donate our proceeds to. Again, of course, we made every decision in consultation with the community. The Ladies of the Loos decided to have a vote and chose three charities: Samaritans, Refuge and Rape Crisis.

In putting together the book we had a lot of support from the other members, which was and is very much appreciated. We really want to thank everyone that we contacted to ask if we could use their advice (see the back of the book), and we do apologise to those we had to cut out for reasons of space.

We have tried to pick out the most useful posts on a range of topics: although there are bound to be things you know already, there's always a new perspective on everything. I'd also like to think that it's a fun book to read because the entries and replies are well written and witty – you could even keep it in your loo!

If you only take one thing away from your time in

the Ladies' Loos it should be a feeling that no-one's perfect, but that it really doesn't matter. We all leave the bedclothes on too long sometimes, we don't always eat what's most healthy, and we definitely don't all go to the gym. The part of the book that sums it all up best for me is 'Living up to the magazines' (in the 'Miscellaneous' chapter). Thank God we're not all Cyborg superwomen, or feel that we have to be. Be positive about your body whatever shape it is, cook what you fancy when you fancy it, leave the washing for another day, but most of all don't beat yourself up about it.

We have also set up a website to go alongside the book – www.theladiesloos.co.uk – where you will find useful links on pretty much anything relating to the book and more. There's also a message board, so if you have any questions or advice, or just want to lurk, you'll be made to feel very welcome.

See you in the Ladies' Loos!

natasha

Beauty

SKIN SCRUBS

Olive oil and sea salt make a great skin scrub.

cookwitch

Soft brown sugar and olive oil also works a treat, and I find it more comfortable than salt! Add whatever essential oils you like to make it smell good!

sushidog

SENSITIVE SKIN

For skin care, if you've got sensitive skin that you want to look great, use Liz Earle. It's only available mail order and from two stores, but it's the best product range I've ever found. Completely natural and invented because she has eczema, it's been wonderful for my skin. www.lizearle.com is the website. The customer service is amazing too and they'll regularly include free items with your purchases.

es

NAILS HELP

I have a silly problem. Well, actually it's a good thing in some ways. I used to bite my nails very badly, but with perseverance and the religious application of nail polish I've stopped and they are now looking pretty good and very long. What I don't know about is what to do when you've had to cut one nail short (I had an accident with a potato peeler a few days ago).

So, should I cut all the nails back to the same length if I have to chop one so they grow evenly, or should I leave my nine pretty nails as they are because the other one will catch up? I'm new to all this manicuring malarkey. What do you do?

lisa g

If I think it doesn't look too daft (it's a thumb or something), I leave the other nine long. Otherwise they all get cut back.

If my nails ever get long enough that I think 'ooh, they're nice and long' there is a 100% chance that I'll break one within 24 hours.

dozle

Personally, I always cut the others to the same length.
If I break it *really* short, I might leave the other a
couple of millimetres longer. I just think it looks really
naff when people have all the nails at different lengths.

fgc

I need some tips to stop biting mine – they are truly
disgusting at the minute and I have bitten them so low
that typing is actually quite painful.

lp

OK, well, this is what's worked for me (and trust me,
I was as bad as you – I've bitten my nails since I was a
kid and they were horrible).
Let's start with what didn't work at all for me:

1. That vile, foul-tasting anti-nail-biting muck that
   gets in food and everywhere! Ugh.
2. Sitting on my hands.
3. Nagging. That makes me worse.
4. Putting bandages on my fingers!

What sort of worked for me was getting false nails put
on. They're too tough to chew (believe me, I tried!)
and it helps to break the habit. I had them on for four
weeks when I got married and it stopped me biting
them for a few months, but not permanently. It did
get me to the stage that I could grow them a couple of
mm though. Next, I got hold of nail clippers, emery
boards, cuticle tips and all that jazz. I used to chew my
cuticles and that got me over that bit.

The turning point, though, was buying a Dior
travel manicure set from the airport and learning to do
a proper manicure. Base coat, colour, topcoat, the

works. I started putting it on religiously. Now the Dior stuff kinda peels off after a day or two, which makes it crap as actual nail polish, but that kind of helped, as I peeled nail polish with my teeth rather than biting them when the urge hit. I kept going, and after a month or so I broke the habit. Now I use a good strong nail polish to keep them strong and take my multivits, and it's all good!

Anyway, that's what worked for me. I hope it's some use.

lisa g

What worked for me was being aware of what I was doing. It requires some willpower – to say 'Hello; I'm biting my nails. I'll stop', rather than just saying 'Oh, nailbiting again. Oh well', and carrying on. After 15 years of biting, that's what worked for me.

meepettemu

NAIL VARNISH REMOVER

Cutex are now doing a conditioning nail varnish remover with nail whitener. I used it to take off dark glossy red polish and there was NO staining at all – and my nails always stain no matter how careful I am or what undercoat I use. A definite 'must buy again' item for me!

cookwitch

UPPER LIP HAIR

I've always had a bit of a moustache, but mostly light enough/sparse enough to ignore. When I was pregnant, and since having my son, it's got much darker and thicker so I started using Jolen bleach on it. Recently, though, I've noticed that the bleach has less effect – it just doesn't seem to lighten the hair anything like as much as it used to. Is it possible my pot of Jolen has gone off in some way? It doesn't have an expiry date on it but I'd guess it's over two years old. (It's the sort where you mix powder from one tub with creme from another to make the gloop you smear on the hair.) Alternatively, what about alternatives... anyone had upper lip wax? I don't find leg waxing painful at all but I can't imagine the same being true on the upper lip. How long would waxing last? Any other thoughts on the matter?

vicky l

I started using Jolen when I was a teen, but as I've got older the hairs have got darker. Since going through early menopause they were just dreadful, so I started getting electrolysis. It's working out pretty well, I have it done every three weeks and it costs £5 for five minutes and she gets loads done in that time. Yes it hurts, but only for a microsecond each hair, and you get used to it. If you can have your legs waxed (and have a child!) then you can stand that pain. And the bonus of this is that after a number of sessions the effects will be permanent.

zoefruitcake

Waxing is a bit ouchy, but not terrible. It lasts several weeks. Trouble is, it tends to give me a couple of spots the day after doing it.

bluedevi

I use these wax-coated strips to remove upper lip hair. It's a bit ouchy and burns afterwards, but I have really sensitive skin. As I only need to do it every four to six weeks, it's not too much of a bother. And well, most of the time I forget about doing it anyway.

I pluck, it's time consuming but I think it's worth it as I have fairly dark colouring so a bright white lip would look daft so I don't bleach. There's always electrolysis, expensive, painful but permanent.

yanata

I've tried electrolysis, but my hirsutism is hormone-based, so if yours has reacted to your hormones being out of whack, the hair may return. Electrolysis is not too painful, but tends to be expensive (here in the US at least).

Why not get a fresh pot, or increase the activator part of the mixture?

mj

SHAVING

Always use conditioner, not shaving foam (too expensive) or soap (ouch!). It leaves the skin softer and makes the hairs easier to shave off.

batswing

Vaseline Lip Balm with aloe vera helps with ye olde shavinge rashe.

cookwitch

COVERING UP SCARS/ TATTOOS

Dermablend comes in every skin tone imaginable. You get a sort of tester set with a little of each till you find the exact match, then send off for the right one – http://www.dermablend.co.uk/ – it is £5 for a sample kit.

moggy

Vitamin E is generally a good thing for your skin, taken orally (in the form of dietary supplements, or just by eating lots of foods which are rich in vitamin E) and applied externally. Try and find a moisturiser that contains vitamin E, or just get some capsules of vitamin E oil, break one open and massage the contents into your skin once a day.

sushidog

IMPROMPTU LIPSTICK

If you can't find your lippy just use a little eyeshadow mixed in with Vaseline, it does the job perfectly and means you can create custom colours that match the rest of your warpaint.

silvernik

EYE MAKE-UP

How does one choose the colours of eyeshadows?
How do you get kohl – pencil eyeliner – to be soft enough to apply instead of simply scratching at your eyelid?

How do you blend colours together without rubbing them off or muddying them both up?

vf

Re: kohl – I think you have to shop around to find a soft one. Other than that, rub the pencil between the palms of your hands to warm it a bit before applying.

sera_squeak

How does one choose the colours of eyeshadows?
Just buy the colours you like. Chances are, they're the same colours as the ones in your wardrobe. And also get a brown day palette, I find it a good basic.
How do you get kohl – pencil eyeliner – to be soft enough to apply instead of simply scratching at your eyelid?
Liquid eyeliner is your friend.
How do you blend colours together without rubbing them off or muddying them both up?
I use my little finger to blend, so I tend to go very lightly. Cream eyeshadows are good to practise with, as they're harder to rub off, and until they dry you're very aware of them so you don't rub too hard.

caturah

How do you get kohl – pencil eyeliner – to be soft enough to apply instead of simply scratching at your eyelid?
Liquid eyeliner is your friend
Now how do you get THAT straight? I always end up with two black eyes...

hazyjayne

I'm utterly terrified of stuff getting too near my eyes (getting contacts in is really fun... so much so I don't do it anymore), so what I tend to do with liquid eyeliner is draw a line, straight as I can, about 1–2 millimetres above my eyelashes. Now obviously, this is going to be seen when I close my eye, so while it's still wet, I smudge it down with a finger towards my eyelashes. End result: a nice straight, deliberately smoky-looking black line.

caturah

I always find liquid eyeliner easy to use, like a felt tip. To get a straight line, follow your lashes, keep the liner as low as possible next to the lashes, and if you need to make it thicker or straighten up the bumps, do it on the second run.

When I do kohl, though, I either finally scratch a thick black line, or then try and smudge it and rub it all off.

uf

If you shop around, you can get proper liquid eyeliner – a tiny brush (like a really small model-painting brush) in the lid, and the remainder full of eyeliner – essentially, like the same set-up as a mascara, but far smaller and with a different brush shape. This is harder to use at first than the 'felt tip'/marker-pen style eyeliners, and certainly will take longer if you're doing dramatic Goth make-up because it's a far thinner tip, but once you get used to it, it's far nicer – and it will never run out on you mid-make-up!

sea_of_flame

You need to choose colours that will compliment your skin. Try and work out what your underlying skin tone is and work from there really The ideal would be to have a play at them all – perhaps go into a big department store and get them to advise you.

Kohl – just choose a soft one and try not to drag it; sometimes feather strokes work well.

Use good-quality brushes. I tend to put a dark colour on the actual lid, a lighter tone above that, with a small amount of highlighter under my brow to lift it. Build the colour up gradually and then when you are happy work along the join to soften the edge. The applicator brush should be reasonably small to allow you to place the colour precisely, but the blending brush should be soft and slightly larger.

clare s

If you have problems with eyeshadow not staying put, may I recommend MAC paint? They do one in a neutral skin shade, in a little tube like oil paints come in. You brush a very small amount over your eyelid, and then apply make-up over the top as normal, and like magic, your make-up stays where you put it and doesn't come off until you try properly to get it off. Fabulous stuff.

A friend of mine used to sharpen her kohl pencil, then briefly flame it with a lighter, then let it cool before applying it. Just sharpening it may help, if there is gunk on the surface of the tip which is making it reluctant to draw?

sushidog

To choose eyeshadows, the best thing is to try them on; a lot of makeup counters in department stores will be happy to do your make-up for you as a demo, and they'll also give you advice about what sort of colours and textures and looks are likely to suit you. Shop around, try lots of different things, decide what you like, and what you're likely to wear.

Eyeliner pencils: some are softer than others. I like Bourjois, as I find the pencils are soft enough to go on easily, but once on they don't smudge too much. Another option is to use a fine (lipliner) brush, damped a little with water or eye cream or any of the various products intended to keep your make-up on for longer (I have an Elizabeth Arden one called, I think, Eye Fix cream, which is great), and a normal powder eye-shadow; this way, you can mix it up to a consistency which goes on easily, it tends to stay on well, and it matches the rest of your make-up perfectly.

Blending: use decent brushes. The Body Shop do very nice brushes which are good quality (I've had some of mine for ten years and they haven't shed at all) and cruelty free (some of the really good-quality ones are made from squirrel hair). A softish brush should be able to blend colours without muddying them. The trick is to go gently and gradually, rather than trying to do it in one stroke.

A good tip taught to me by a nice man at MAC: sweep a light shade across the whole eyelid. Then take a darker shade, and make a filled-in triangle in the outer corner of the lid; the bottom of the triangle follows the top lashes from the corner to about a third of the way in, and the point of the triangle is in the crease of the eyelid above the corner of the eye. Now, using a soft blending brush, gently blend the dark colour inwards a bit, to soften the edges of the triangle. Quick, easy, works with lots of different colour combinations, looks fab!

sushidog

1. I have a basic stock of neutral eye shadows for quick everyday wear and a whole load of VERY bold stage make-up colours for when I fancy something different and harder wearing.

    There are no set rules about what colours you can and can't wear – it's just a case of deciding what look you want to achieve and what feels comfortable/suits.

2. You can achieve the same effect by using a damp angled brush and a dark shadow instead. With this method, you have far more control over the application and it's easier to blend.

3. Practise, practise, practise, and invest in a set of good-quality brushes from the Body Shop or similar – they make all the difference.

    Prime your eyelids with foundation, then experiment with different methods of application. For example, I will often apply one dry colour over my whole eyelid then, using a damp brush and a different colour, pick out areas to highlight. Through different application techniques you can achieve very different results.

pipistrellus

Virgin Vie do a very lovely soft eye pencil – it's fantastic, you just have to go near the eye with it to make a mark – and is available in the standard greys, blacks, blues. It's plastic, though, not wood, so you need one of their special pencil sharpeners.

kauket

Re kohl, I use twist-up pencils from Avon. They are really soft and don't need sharpening, and cost only £4.50.

pp

GETTING ADVICE ON MAKE-UP

Take a friend and go to the make-up counter of a big department store. They'll give you advice (often very good) but will also try to sell you stuff that may or may not be necessary – the friend is there to tell you what really looks good. It can be a really good way to learn make-up tricks and techniques, and it doesn't cost you anything unless you buy the products afterwards; I often head down to Selfridge's if I've got a big night out, and have a play around.

elle

Go to high-end make-up counters (Chanel, Dior, YSL, MAC etc.) in department stores, and ask for advice. They are generally quite happy to be helpful, particularly if you haven't chosen the busiest times to ask. I've always found MAC helpful wherever I went;

other places seem to vary, so pick someone who looks friendly! Bear in mind that it's quite acceptable to try make-up on and then leave without buying anyway; after all, you'll want to see how it looks in natural light, and how well it lasts. If you can't get them to help you by just turning up, you could try booking an appointment; they can be expensive, but usually you can redeem the cost against products. However, this is a bit limiting.

A lot of places do palettes of perhaps four or five colours that work well together, but can also be worn separately, so one of those might be a good start. Urban Decay do some called Face Cases, which have four eyeshadows, four lipsticks or glosses, and either a blusher or a highlighter, and the packaging includes some instructions on how to wear it.

Another option is to arrange a make-up playdate with some of your more make-up-minded friends: ask them to bring their make-up over and show you what they think would work on you! You may not like everything they suggest, but it should give you some ideas, and it's fun!

sushidog

I second this. On sushidog's advice I had a make-up lesson at the MAC in Neal Street (not free at £20, but I got it for Christmas and the full amount is redeemable against their lovely make-up). The make-up artist helps you pick colours for whatever look you want to go for (I chose 'polished office look'), shows you how to do everything on your face, and then shows you again on a face diagram that you can take home and tape to your mirror while you try and remember what tube #19 was for. Worth the money

– I feel like I know what I'm doing with make-up now, and that makes me feel confident enough to forget about the make-up and concentrate on the meeting/conference/presentation at hand.

easterbunny

ORAL PIERCINGS

If you are getting an oral piercing, arrange to meet friends (for it or immediately after) to go for ice-cream/sorbet.

kimkali

HELP!!

I need a foolproof way of concealing love bites before I get in serious trouble!

mendi

I used to find make-up never worked terribly well – try roll-necks and/or carefully draped silk scarves! Then train the culprit to either stop leaving them, or to leave them somewhere they won't show.

sea_of_flame

Contract a nasty rash and hide them that way!

darth tigger

Toothpaste. Put toothpaste on it, leave for about 15 minutes, then get the brush and rub it gently.

fgc

MAKE-UP SITE

http://www.saveonmakeup.co.uk
This site is pretty good and no shipping charges either. They do have some things that are regularly available, but I don't really bank on them always having what I want – they do have some good deals sometimes though.

cookwitch

MYSTERIOUS NAIL POLISH BUBBLES

I seem to have this curious problem of bubbles appearing in the finish whenever I try to paint my nails. At first, I thought that it was simply my

fault. **For various reasons, I've never worn any until recently, and had little idea on how it's supposed to be done. Then I thought it was the paint itself, nabbed by the handful in the cheapie discontinued bin.**

After several weeks of disappointment, I decided to try again. Although the added expense solved the breakage and chipping problems, I still can't seem to get rid of these damnable bubbles! Again, I assumed it was me. I tried to be far more careful this last time and still, more bubbles than ever. When I asked some of the ladies around work, they were equally perplexed.

tess flynn

I get that too, so no, it's not your fault! I found that when I use a base coat, it seems to stop it. I use a ridge filler/base coat, the kind that you get in a three-step French manicure, and that seems to have solved the problem.

cookwitch

Try buffing your nails before applying the polish, and then washing your hands before starting. This will smooth out the surface. Then apply a nail conditioner of some type (painting your nails is actually ludicr-ously bad for them, so I like to put something under-neath as some kind of sop to 'yeah, poor baby nails, now shut up and drown under lacquer for a while'). Anyway, now you want to apply a base coat. A clear nail polish will do for this – it will also prevent your coloured lacquer discolouring your nails when you take it off – but I think some make-up companies also do special base coats. Try a few out and see what's right for you. Wait for that to dry completely (leave it about ten minutes) and apply a single coat of your chosen polish over the top. To do this, shake the bottle, and then apply three strokes to each nail. Each stroke runs from the cuticle at the back to the tip of the nail. I usually go middle, left side, right side, but that's personal preference. The reason you're getting bubbles is probably:

- Applying too thickly
- Over-stroking
- Applying unevenly
- Air in the polish (don't pump the brush when recharging!).

Getting your nails smooth (which the buffing and the base coat will do) will go some way to stopping you needing to apply thickly, should prevent the stuff going on unevenly, and will remove the need for over-stroking, so should help get rid of the bubbles (although not guaranteed!). Anyway, wait for your colour to dry and then you can either apply a second layer, or pop a topcoat on.

Usually when I paint my nails with standard lacquers (I tend to use express-finish stuff these days 'cause I just can't be arsed), it would take me about 40 minutes to do properly, with a base coat, three layers of colour and then a topcoat. I could wear that lot for a week, go to the gym, shower etc., and it wouldn't chip. Which is either testimony to the brilliance of Boots Natural Collection make-up as was, or the sheer awesome power of my application techniques. Probably the former, but every little helps.

easternpromise

I've been told that it's a result of oil on your nails. So, yeah, base coat. You should always do a base coat, to protect your nails, and a topcoat to protect the finish, anyway.

fgc

I also find that it happens when I don't let my nails dry thoroughly before applying the next coat.

redshira

MASCARA

I have an internal job interview coming up and I have brought some make-up in order to try to make myself look presentable.

I seldom wear make-up: in fact, it will be the first time I have worn make-up to work in the two years that I have worked here. My problem is with mascara: whenever I use it, my eyelashes end up imprinting mascara on my eyelids, making a mess and filling me with despair and futility (OK, so not that bad, but it is annoying). Has anyone got any tips on how to avoid this happening?

tooth_fairy

Sweep the brush from side to side, just once each
way. If you do the forward brushing it tends to clog up.

aellia

Apply mascara, then take a folded tissue and hold it
near your eye while you blink; this gets rids of the
excess.

sushidog

I used to apply it, then brush through with a washed
mascara brush to remove icky bits and excess. I can
also remember holding tissue against my upper eyelid
and brushing the eyelashes back against the tissue to
remove smears.

ailbhe

I wipe most of the mascara off the applicator with a bit
of loo roll before I apply it.

moggy

TWEEZERS

**To save my eyebrows and moustache going wild,
can you recommend me a good pair of tweezers?
The Boots ones have a pointy tip and I didn't
really like them. I also don't like the slanty ones.**

**I've never bought expensive tweezers. Is it
worth paying the extra money?**

anna

I always used to think that tweezers were just tweezers – why bother paying more? Then I used my flatmate's Tweezermans and there's just no going back! Plucking is an entirely (well, maybe not *entirely*) new experience. They do a number of different tips – I use slanty for getting more than one hair at a time, and pointy (you could have someone's eye out with 'em!) for individual hairs. *Definitely* worth the expense.

cm

I love my Tweezermans and wouldn't go back to any others for anything. I have the slanted ones, so I have a little pointy bit for finishing off, and the flatter edge for large-scale tweezing. They will sharpen them free of charge for you and they have a long guarantee on them as well.

nikki

One day later... Just bought some slanted Tweezermans after all of your advice yesterday and I will never use anything else. They are fab.

anna

FOUNDATION

I use Maybelline Dream Matte Mousse foundation, that's great for skin. And you don't have to use a lot to get a good spread – I've had the pot six months now and it still looks full.

beautifulcreep

I use Savlon to start with, like a base coat on all the cracked/dry bits, then foundation: works a treat.

smallblakflower

MASCARA AND OTHER SUCH GIRLINESS

What, in your opinion, is the best type of mascara? I have pretty average lashes in terms of length, thickness and curliness, but I curl them, so am more interested in length and thickness than curl. Main problems I have with mascaras are: gloopiness, flaking off quickly (usually with anything that has a white undercoat type thing), and being a bit too dry so they don't go on smoothly.

lm

Benefit do the best cosmetics I've ever used: their 'Bad Gal' mascara is definitely the best on the market.

madeleine

I have tried so many, and the best was always L'Oreal Volume Mascara, which gave me false black lashes so

large I could sweep the floor with them. Then I found
a different L'Oreal Lash Architect mascara in brown,
which is such a nice consistency and looks so natural
that I'll never have anything else again.

I've tried a lot of mascaras, and they're either wet
and sticky (Maybelline), or they stick all the lashes
together (Avon) or they're clumpy (Rimmel) or
something else (everything else). And mascaras aren't
cheap!

uf

BLISTERS

Blister advice anyone?

**I wore some boots today that I haven't worn in
a while and they used to be comfy. I managed to
get to work okay and then they started to hurt,
so I spent all day pottering about in my socks. Of
course I had to wear the damned things home
again, so I now have a good old blister on my
right heel. I've never had one as I wear sensible
shoes (usually). I had to pierce it a little as it had
swollen up, but what do I do with it now?**

cookwitch

Compeed blister plasters are fantastic.

westernind

I know it's too late, but you shouldn't pierce a blister – it could become infected. The blister fluid is your body's way of protecting the injury underneath.

suzylou

If you *have* to pierce it, try to bathe your foot in a strong salt water solution afterwards and then stick a blister plaster on it quickly.

ailbhe

Blisters heal a lot faster if wiped with surgical spirit, which is then allowed to dry.

kimkali

CELLULITE ADVICE

According to *Slimming* magazine the best cellulite-beaters are caffeine, co-enzyme Q10, juniper/lavender/rosemary essential oils, and isoproteins (derived from soya beans).

Personally I've never found anything that gets rid of it completely, but dry brushing, Lush's Buffy the Backside Slayer (which I use on my arms, bum, tum and thighs) used every other day, with the other days using a firming gel, help keep it to a minimum. I use a Chinese Tea gel with Sargasso Seaweed, but the one recommended by *Slimming* is Nivea Body Sculpting and Smoothing Cream.

loulou

HANDCREAM QUESTION

- Can anyone recommend for me a handcream that has the following:
- A reasonable sun protection factor
- Made by a company with a FCOD (fixed cut off date for animal testing on ingredients)
- Good for sensitive (but not overly so) skin
- Is reasonably good without me having to sell all my possessions in order to pay for it?

tooth_fairy

Simple's anti-aging with SPF protection hand cream is good. According to the FAQs on their website they do not test on animals and they do not used animal-derived ingredients.

isobel

LIP BALM RECOMMENDATION

I always use Crabtree and Evelyn's lip conditioner. It works really well and you don't need to keep topping it up because one application lasts ages. It has SPF factor 15 too!

moggy

COMPASSIONATE SHOPPING

Information from *The Compassionate Shopping Guide* produced by Naturewatch.

FCOD

There is no legal requirement to test finished products on animals (personal care or household), yet newly developed ingredients do have to be tested on animals to fulfil EU legislative requirements. Every year 7000 animals are used and then euthanased for this purpose – the real cost of innovation.

Companies that have a fixed cut-off date (FCOD) policy won't use any of the newly developed ingredients that have been subject to animal testing after a specific date. The company nominates this date and insists their suppliers comply.

Companies that commit to the FCOD policy forgo the competitive advantage that might be gained from using newly developed ingredients.

Five-year rolling rule

Companies adopting a five-year rolling rule only restrict the ingredients they use to those that have not been tested on animals in the past five years. This approach leaves the door open for newly developed ingredients and does little to discourage animal testing.

Some well-known brands with an FCOD (note this list is not exhaustive – also in the case of supermarkets refers to own-brand products only)

ALDI (cosmetics not household)
Betterware
Bio-D
Clarins
Co-op
Holland & Barrett
Iceland
John Lewis
King of Shaves
KwikSave
Lush (In fact Lush will buy no ingredients that have any link to animal testing, so technically do not have a FCOD)
Molton Brown
Netto
New Look
Next
Nisa Today's (Budgens, Costcutter, Londis)
Sainsburys (cosmetics not household)
Somerfield
Waitrose (cosmetics, not household)
Weleda

If you would like more information or would like to get a copy of the Compassionate Shopping guide, go to www.naturewatch.org

SWEATING

Ugh.

I sweat. A lot. Just under my arms. Which means I can't wear light tops, I can't wear tight-fitting tops. I can't wear anything except black, or thick tops. And I use that driclor stuff. I put it on this morning and waited for it to dry. I'm still sitting here in jeans and a bra. And I just feel a trickle run down my arm. Jesus, it's not even hot, and I'm STILL sweating. What can I do?

meepettemu

No no no... you put it on before you go to bed and wash it off in the morning. Then use normal deodorant for the day. It works, honest. My wardrobe isn't *entirely* made up of black anymore. Use for about a week and then you should be able to cut back to once every two or three nights. However, I kind of plan my wardrobe now and only use it if I'm going to be wearing certain tops the next day.

kl

I use Mitchum, which has always been good for me. I'm a, uh, glower too, and I tend to only be able to use a deodorant for a couple of weeks before it stops working, but Mitchum has been brilliant. If neither works, then consider seeing your GP. There are treatments for excess sweating you can have, including (believe it or not!) Botox!

lozette

SUNCREAM

Does anyone here know of a suncream that a) does not feel horrid and greasy on my poor little already-greasy face, and b) is not some tensquillion quid Laboratoire Gainyourmoney stuff?

bee

Decent sunscreen *is* pricey. It's worth buying a moisturiser and/or foundation with an SPF in it, as that will give you some basic protection without feeling like you've got extra gloop on your face.

sushidog

This: http://www.p20.co.uk Honestly, it really works. It is on the pricey side, but it lasts for ages and you don't need to put as much of the stuff on (it's a clear slightly oily liquid, not a cream, and it seems to go a long way), and you really do only need to put it on once in the morning, so it's economical, honest. I normally burn really easily (I got sunburnt in London, in April this year) but this stuff lasted for a whole day of walking up mountains in Switzerland in midsummer!

janet mcknight

Piz Buin do a stick that's specifically for your face and only costs about £8 or so. Different texture because it's not a lotion so perhaps not as thick and greasy.

sera_squeak

SKIN CARE REGIMES

It's your duty to be beautiful!

This weekend I realised that I'd totally been neglecting myself, and as a result I had very dry skin on my legs and arms. I decided to have a bath (which I don't do often – I'm a shower person) and although I thought I had all the right girly products in the cupboard. I didn't, so I ended up exfoliating myself with... a kitchen scourer. Classy.

This got me thinking about the idea of 'health and beauty', and about how it's easy, sometimes, to get caught up in marketing and to buy into the ideas of beauty that companies sell. I tend to buy a fair few beauty products, but I end up not using them because I don't really have a beauty routine. I guess I'm a bit of a sucker for the promises that products make, and the packaging, and so on.

I just wondered whether other ladies here had particular regimes or products that they're devoted to, whether you buy lots of beauty

products, or not many. Would you die if you had to leave the house without make-up, for example? Will you only use one particular type of moist-uriser? Or are you at the opposite end of the scale and consciously avoiding the health/beauty hype?

tb

I'm devoted to almost nothing. I'll use make-up for parties and stuff, but that's about it. It's not a conscious avoidance, more general laziness – if I can have an extra 15 minutes' sleep in the morning, people can see me without make-up.

About the only products I am addicted to are hair-care products – Andrew Collinge moisturising shampoo/conditioner. But even then I'll vary it a bit.

lannie

I'm pretty much a no-routine kinda gal. My face gets washed in the shower with the rest of me (with a shower gel selected for smelling nice), I only moisturise if my skin feels dry (rarely), and I wear make-up maybe twice a year. My haircare routine is wash/comb/leave, although I sometimes use leave-in conditioner or curl activator stuff if I happen to not be running late. Oh, but I don't use soap – it leaves my skin feeling horrid.

I decided to wear full, albeit fairly natural, make-up for my wedding, for the first time ever, and I had to get the girl in Boots to explain about foundation/concealer/powder to me. Apparently the effect was quite good, but I can't imagine having the time and lack of laziness to do all that every day! The make-up I wear on run-of-the-mill special occasions, if I have time and can be bothered, is eyeliner, mascara, neutral-ish eyeshadow and lipstick.

ej

The only 'product' that plays a role in my life is Clearasil Facial Wash 3in1 (the cream, not the gel). It's a scrub with antiseptic goodness that helps prevent spots. I use it as a sort of face mask before washing it off.

secretrebel

Being vegan and extremely aware of the immense suffering that animals go through to bring most 'beauty' products to the shelves of stores, I have a very simple routine. I wash my face in the shower with Dr Bronners baby soap or Avalon Organics Lavender face scrub. If my face is not looking good I use a Native American witch hazel blend as a toner. For make-up I use Alba Terra Tints on my lips (organic, cruelty-free, tinted chapstick) and occasionally a cruelty-free mascara that I got from the local health food store. That's it.

lahermite

LUSH LUSH LUSH LUSH LUSH LUSH LUSH LUSH (http://www.lush.co.uk)

Everything they make is vegetarian, and much is vegan. No animal testing. All goodness.

I am a bath junkie.

Oh right, my routine. Warning, this will look like an ad for Lush:

Evening bath, usually with a bath bomb/bubble bar from Lush, or occasionally Radox bubbles or maybe a bath bead from the Body Shop. I wouldn't have a bath without some sort of smelly/bubbly/salt/bead thing in.

If I didn't have an evening bath, I have a morning shower.

I wash my face with Fresh Farmacy (http://www.lush.co.uk/pages/freshfar.html) and in the shower I use any of Lush's shower gels on a pair of exfoliating gloves, which I use every day (I think I got them from the Body Shop, but you can get them anywhere). I wash and condition my hair daily too.

Out of the shower I lotion up with Dream Cream (http://www.lush.co.uk/pages/dreamcre.html) and I moisturise my face. I'm currently using a freebie moisturiser from Boots No. 5 range, but I don't like it as much as Cosmetic Lad (http://www.lush.co.uk/pages/cosmetic.html).

About once every ten days or so I use a facial mask, and when I think about it I use a hair mask (maybe once every six weeks? I should do it more often though).

I have my eyebrows waxed and eyelashes and eye-brows tinted every few weeks – actually, I'm out of the habit of that at the moment because of lack of cash, but I'm about to be rich again.

I used to have a manicure regularly, but I do it myself (not as well) these days. I use a cuticle cream and a beeswax hand cream from Burt's Bees daily.

If I get around to it in the morning, I wear con-cealer, eyeliner, mascara, and lip gloss daily, and I dry my hair out straight.

offensive_mango

FRIZZY HAIR

Vaseline! MUCH better and cheaper than any specialist product. Smooth some over your hands, then through your hair, avoiding the roots.

mc

LEG HAIR

So now I have the problem which I have every summer. Do I grow hairs long enough for waxing, which means that's it for me being able to have bare legs this year and retreat back into 40 denier tights, or do I undo all the good work that waxing does and just slash at my legs with a razor until they're a worn-and-bleeding but hair-free mess?

brane

Your stubble doesn't have to be very long for waxing: generally about three days' growth is fine!

sushidog

I wear trousers as soon as I start getting hairy, and if exposed leg hair suddenly becomes evident I just declare I like it better that way and dare anyone to disagree with me.

tooth_fairy

I brave the waxing suite, can't do it myself, don't believe any of those Veet adverts.

quorta

Charing Cross hospital has a lovely, cheap beauty salon for public use...

genie22

I hack at mine with a razor. This generally makes my knees bleed, which can be quite embarrassing if I have to shave just before I leave the house. I tried to wax once, somehow took off the skin and left the hair behind. Decided not to do that again.

suzylou

I bought that there Immac Rasera thingy that gives you a plastic looks-like-a-razor palette thingy and a can of odd-smelling evil chemicals. They say it takes three minutes... and it really does and it lasts for ages (though probably not as long as they say it does), and when it grows back it feels a bit softer because the hair's been dissolved rather than cut (same effect as waxing). I am extremely happy with it (don't know if it's a viable solution for you though). I tried home waxing last year and salon waxing once, but I (and they) always miss bits so I have to shave the strips they miss anyway.

jinn

DEALING WITH ACNE SPOTS

Tea tree oil has always helped
me with acne. It doesn't smell
great but it works. Twice a day,
wipe your face with it after washing.
Bioré (I think) do spot-reducing
strips that you leave on overnight
which reduce swelling. Medicated
foundation can help as well.

cookwitch

Short-term fix: go get a salon facial. It can really help.
   Long-term: I have sort of deep, cystic spots.
Unfortunately I have trouble controlling them, as
they don't really come to the surface so can't be
squeezed or exfoliated away. But do invest in a good
skincare routine (I used to use Clinique but can't
afford it at the moment; Garnier do a decent sub-
stitute. I also recommend St Ives anti-zit apricot scrub
in the white tube). Also drink lots of water, and get a
topical cream like Quinoderm to use when you have
an outbreak.

lozette

Lush's Fresh Farmacy – dab some on the spot (I usually put it quite thick, like a mini mask) and leave it to dry, at least ten minutes. Sometimes I've left it on overnight if it's a bad one. It helps clear out the muck so the spot can start healing. Fresh Farmacy is a really good cleanser generally for problem skin, I've found.

Lush also do a face mask called Cosmetic Warrior, which has helped my skin clear up when I've neglected it for a bit (I go through lazy periods, especially when busy/tired, i.e. when I need it the most, when I don't practise what I'm about to preach).

I found the best long-term treatment for spots was just to get into the habit of using a good-quality cleanser, toner, and moisturiser, every day, morning and night. Most of the stuff I use nowadays is Lush, so it doesn't have to be expensive, but I find it keeps my spots to a minimum. The trick is finding the right combination of products that work for your skin, and that can take time.

silke

I find that sweating really improves my skin. After a week of heavy exercise my skin was positively glowing from all the nasties I sweated out. Maybe you could try going to a steam room or sauna and you might get some really good results. Some people get more spots initially as the skin cleans itself out (I didn't), but it won't be long at all before it gets better. Maybe a more long-term solution?

siren

I started using 'Acne Getaway 101e' the other week and it's helped a lot. Most of the problem was cleared up within a week and it is very good at stopping the new spots from developing into huge pussy messes. You can get it at Chinese herb shops – it costs about £20– £25. A friend got some through eBay and it was about £8 including post and packaging. I have no idea why or how it works, but it's been miraculous for me. I had been using Oxy 5 and the like, which really dried out my skin. The Acne Getaway stuff doesn't dry it at all.

elethe

I had nasty, lumpy, painful acne around my jawline when I was 22/23, and not at all any more. What worked for me was:

1. Going to the doctor. He recommended Panoxy Gel, which is evil stuff with peroxide in it, which you can buy over the counter in Boots. I used it twice a day, and it dried my skin out (I have very sensitive, dry, eczema-prone skin) in a scary way without improving the acne.

2. Before I went back to the doctor to ask for something else, I decided to use it *for two weeks*, following the instructions on the packet *to the letter* – which meant using it sparingly once a day. I used it just before bed (bleached my pillows a bit, so don't sleep on expensive ones!) and never, ever in the morning.

3. Because I have such dry skin, I also completely downgraded and simplified washing my face: no fancy products, just washing it morning and night with aqueous cream (an emollient rather than a soap) and plain water, and then moisturising (aqueous cream to moisturise before going to

bed, a basic Nivea one with a light SPF during the day).

4. And two weeks later, all my nasty horrible deep spots had gone. They've never come back, either; since then, I've had the occasional spot here or there, but they are overwhelmingly the shallow, non-painful, superficial kind. If I ever do get a deep spot, it's completely isolated and heals fairly quickly with a tiny little bit of Panoxy stuff.

Other people probably don't have quite such dry skin as me, so they might not need to reject soap altogether in favour of aqueous cream. I would suggest junking expensive and complicated cleansers and making your cleansing routine mostly water + moisturiser, though. You'll need something to shift a bit of grease and any make-up, but then wash whatever that is off with water. You also might not need to moisturise at night – my girlfriend doesn't – but you should in the morning. That 'dry, tight' feeling that a lot of people associate with 'clean' skin is supposedly pretty bad for it.

la bias

VITAMIN E LOTIONS

I've recently come off really strong steroids for facial palsy, and apart from a gamut of unpleasant side effects, the wretched pills have brought me out in acne!

Twice daily scrubbing with Johnson's Clean and Clear seems to be wresting some kind of control back over my flesh, but the steroids will take a while to clear my system and in the meantime another of their effects is they slow down my body's ability to heal itself (especially in the annoying pimple department). I don't want to end up scarred as well as bad tempered, so I thought any lotions to help my skin rejuvenate might be an idea.

Anyone had any luck with the vitamin E lotions? Or anything else? It's healing and anti-scarring I'm after rather than spot blitzing. Any recommendations? I have sensitive skin and can't be doing anything with Tea Tree oil in it (that stuff brings me up in a hideous, weeping rash!).

md

Aloe vera is supposed to be good for healing and anti-scarring, and certainly did wonders for my recent bad sunburn – normally I'd be peeling and bleeding for ages, but I practically bathed in aloe vera and the skin was all pink and healthy-looking after a week. (NB: go for something that is mostly aloe vera, i.e. not just 'contains a bit of aloe vera' cleanser etc. – usually comes as a colourless gel and absorbs really well, doesn't leave any stickiness/greasiness etc.). I usually get aloe vera from health food shops as they seem to do it in larger quantities, but you can probably get it in Boots etc.

janet mcknight

Cocoa butter is supposed to be good for healing scars, stretch marks etc. Currently slapping it on my huge stretch-marked nine-month-pregnant belly in the hope of this... Palmers is really good, smells kinda chocolatey!

ladyynara

Sounds like aloe vera might well be your best bet, but if you want to give vitamin E a try, you can buy vitamin E oil capsules; before bed, pierce one with a needle or the point of a sharp knife, squeeze out the oil and apply to scarred areas. I used vitamin E when I got my nipple pierced (with some Tea Tree as well), and it healed quickly and cleanly.

sushidog

Lavender oil is very good for healing skin complaints.

sesquipedality

For healing things, I don't think Hypercal cream can be beaten at all. Shuts wounds up in no time. I would say vitamin E is more for scar prevention after the wounds have healed.

bee

ELECTRO-LYSIS

Right, talk to me about electrolysis. I've finally got fed up with my moustache, which was OK-ish until I went through pregnancy, when it got much darker and thicker. I have been bleaching it, but I'm not happy with a) the faff b) the results and c) how long it lasts.

I've pretty much decided to go for electrolysis. I've read the scare stories so I know it's important to pick a properly qualified person, and I know the results and the number of sessions needed are variable depending on regrowth patterns etc.

What I'm interested in is:

- Any recommendations for a place who will do a decent job
- Any tips for making it less painful/more effective
- Any idea as to the likely long-term cost? It seems to be around £10 for a five-minute session, but I've no idea how many sessions would be required. One website I found implied it would add up to about £250 total: does that sound about right?
- Anything else relevant.

vicky l

The laser fan club!

I'm partway through a series of laser treatments for facial hair, and so far my experience is good. I've been going to Lasercare, who don't have a clinic in Cambridge. I asked my GP to recommend somewhere, which she was happy to do even though it wasn't an NHS procedure – I suggest you do the same.

Because it depends on the pigment in the hair to carry the heat to the root, laser treatment works best when there's a strong contrast between the colour of the skin and the unwanted hair. From your user icons, I'm guessing your unwanted hair is quite a bit darker than your skin, which would probably make you a good candidate.

Melanin (the stuff that makes us tan) tends to gather around the treatment site, which can cause skin discoloration – essentially an area that's more tanned than the surrounding skin. Clinics are therefore unwilling to treat tanned skin, as it's likely to get even darker (which also reduces the contrast between the skin and hair colour). They also advise using strong sunblock on treated skin, as this helps to prevent these areas tanning faster than the rest of you. The literature also warns that tenderness and swelling are possible side effects, and advises using a cooling aloe vera lotion.

Having tried both, I've found laser treatment considerably less painful than electrolysis. On my neck and chin I haven't felt much at all – no more than a slight tingle. On my upper lip, the treatment does hurt – something like being pricked very quickly with a very sharp pin, or (as the brochures always say) having a thin rubber band flicked against my skin. But the pain is momentary and the treatment very quick – a couple of minutes at most, and only a few seconds for the upper lip.

I have sort of mid-pale skin – I do tan, but tend to

burn unless I use sunblock. I've been using SPF35 (Ambre Solaire kids – smells like passion fruit!) on the treated areas and have had no discoloration. I've also had no swelling or soreness – by the time I've walked to the front desk to book my next appointment the only lasting effect is the smell of burned hair (which kind of sticks in my nostrils for half an hour or so).

The fine dark hairs on my upper lip and all the dark hairs on my chin and neck are completely gone after two treatments. The paler, more bristly hairs on my chin and neck are proving more stubborn, but the clinic are turning the laser up a little every time I go and are confident they can get the majority. I'll have to mop up the rest (the grey ones!) with electrolysis, or keep plucking them.

I'm a convert (can you tell?) and feel the £350 for my course of six treatments is money well spent.

wey

How many sessions depends on how resilient the hair is. I started going every couple of weeks and now I'm down to every few months. My moustache hasn't reappeared for ages, but some chin hairs keep rearing their ugly heads.

I wouldn't recommend using local anaesthesia. It certainly would numb the area, but that could mean that too much is done in one session and the after-pain much greater. The first woman to do mine had a story of a lady who had a numbed lip and she was red and sore for ages afterwards.

My personal experience is that it hurts a lot for a few milliseconds and hardly at all afterwards.

kate atkin-wright

THREAD VEINS

I have horrible thread veins on my thighs. I never bothered much about them as I always wore trousers, but lately I've taken to wearing short skirts again and now I'm really conscious of them. Not helped by my partner asking me the other day, what's that bruise on your leg? Aargh! Patch of veins! Aargh!

What do I DO??

cookwitch

I ignore them and pretend they are not there. It's the simplest and cheapest method.

dozle

Get some tattoos to cover them! A dragon curving around your thigh or something.

caroline

Fishnets look good, cover a surprising amount of blemishes, and aren't uncomfortably hot. Or stockings and suspenders, for added sexiness.

dorian

I was amazed to find that thread veins can be removed using a saline solution. You inject a tiny amount into

the veins and they close up and disappear! (Only to be
done professionally, obviously.)

pipistrellus

WAXING

**I'd like to canvass your opinions on waxing. I've
always been too much of a wimp to try it; however, it's summer, I'm 2½ stone lighter than I
was last year, and I want to show my legs off!
Shaved them at the weekend and discovered a
day or so later I'd completely missed my knees,
plus they're going stubbly again already. So how
painful is it really? And would you recommend
doing it at home or going to a salon?**

cazmanian minx

Waxing isn't too bad if you take a painkiller about 45
minutes before you go for the first time.

I'd go to a salon first time so you can see how it's
done. It's also less messy.

genie22

Nuts to wax. Honey is the answer. Put a couple of
tablespoons of honey in a pan and heat it gently, then
pour it on to a plate and allow to cool until you can
scoop it up together into a sticky ball (it takes a while
to get the right consistency – if it's too soft and sticky
just pop it back in the pan and heat a bit more; if it's
too hard then you need to start again). Anyway, once

you have the ball, roll over legs, arms and other areas.
The hair will come straight out and your legs will taste
of honey. Yum!

I rarely do this as it takes a while and can be messy,
but in my experience it works far better than any
home waxing kit I've ever tried.

And who says being half-Egyptian doesn't have its
perks?

easternpromise

HOW TO WHITEN DIS-COLOURED TEETH

Phillips' Sonicare toothbrushes offer a
28-day whiter teeth guarantee or your
money back. I've got one but have
never used it enough to know if it
works – I have also had a lot of cosmetic
dentistry anyway, thanks to smashing my
mouth up repeatedly when I was little, so
I wouldn't notice on my front teeth as
they're all at least half fake anyway.

sara

You could change your tea. My mother raves about Redbush tea. It has no tannin in it, which is I think what stains your teeth. I tried it, it's very nice and is caffeine-free too.

kg

SPOTTY UPPER ARMS

Possibly a weird question, but I've had teeny-tiny lumps on the outside of my upper arms for as long as I can remember now. Recently I've become a bit more fixated on them and so I've taken to scratching at them (though I should point out that they aren't itchy), picking at them, squeezing them – and of course thereby making the whole thing look worse, all red and scratched and stuff. I'm kind of assuming they are spots of the common-or-garden variety, given that when I squeeze them between my fingernails, white stuff comes out. But they don't behave like the spots I had when I was a teen/have before my period, in that they never 'ripen' to the stage where I could squeeze them more safely. I try to scrub them with exfoliator in the shower, but they aren't getting better.

bee

I get them too, and have been assured that they are oily deposits under the skin. I find that they get worse if I allow them to see sunlight (I also get them on my face). There's no harm in them, as you have already noticed they don't grow or pus or do other spotlike things, and once the oil is popped out of them they go away. I'd suggest using sunblock/high factor if you don't want them to recur.

am

Possibly keratosis pilaris (http://www.aocd.org/skin/ dermatologic_diseases/keratosis_pilaris.html) – it's really common. I have them too! I use an anti-spot shower gel (Superdrug have a good own-brand one in a blue bottle) and exfoliate gently to keep them at bay. Something else I've noticed – my spots have reduced even more since I started using a moisturising shower gel (lots of other people here have suggested moisturising lots). I use Johnsons Baby Softwash, which is great. My arms used to be a mess of those spots too, but nowadays they're not bad at all.

lozette

There's a genetic component to that: my family is prone to them. They are the result of very small pores in fine skin becoming blocked with dead skin cells. Two months of exfoliation and moisturising every day and you will see a massive improvement. One of those 'scrubs' that you get in pampering sets will also do the job, as will those sea sponge things that you can get from Boots and the Body Shop. The sea sponge is probably the best.

As you don't get moisturising with the exfoliation unless you use Buffy, you will need to moisturise with something non-greasy. Palmers' Cocoa Butter

Formula is very good, for this in particular. That's the formula that smells less strongly than the cocoa butter itself.

juggzy

EPILATOR

I recently bought an epilator. Anyone want to share any tips to lessen the probably inevitable screaming agony of it all?

bee

The pain gets less well, painful, with each use.

Exfoliate to prevent ingrowing hairs.

Mine has a cooling attachment that you are supposed to freeze, but I can't get along with it as it won't work unless my skin is dry, and obviously the melting attachment leaves moisture.

One thing I find is that it can take AGES. I mean I did my legs last night and it took 45 minutes to do the lot. But I don't know if that is just me.

It can take a while to get used to, but personally I think it is worth sticking with it. My friend always takes a couple of paracetamol about an hour beforehand, but I've never needed that. Oddly enough, I've also found that one leg hurts more than the other. If you find that then remember to do that one first.

zoefruitcake

I honestly don't find mine too painful. Use a gentle start attachment first if it has one, don't try to do it immediately after moisturising (leaves unpleasant gunk in the epilator), and exfoliate well to prevent ing-rowing hairs (though I've only really had problems with that when doing my bikini line). Using a cooling pack or something equivalent afterwards might be handy the first time.

lisa g

NATURAL DEODORANT

My mother swears by a lemon, cut in half and rubbed under her arms; she says that it lasts longer than a day and works better than deodorant. She simply cuts off the old slice every morning.

land_girl

KEEPING CLEAN AT FESTIVALS

Hi Ladies,
   I'm off to Reading Festival and won't be able to wash for about three or four nights.  **Now I like to be clean, and as I am prone to thrush I particularly like to be clean when it's hot. I'm a bit concerned about it cropping up while I'm there due to not being able to shower.**
   Do you think taking some Femfresh wipes or similar would be a good idea? I've heard bad things about them disturbing pH balances and so on, but I can't imagine not washing down there for more than a day!

af

There are usually showers that you can use, but I'd suggest simple Johnson's baby wipes – anything designed for babies is far less likely to cause you a problem. Also, it's a good idea to buy a small pack of them and keep it in your bag during the day with some loo roll. Don't expect the toilets to have any, or to be able to wash your hands properly.

silverixnay

Baby wipes are very good and the Johnson's unper-
fumed ones are nice and gentle. Also, take a tube of
Canesten with you just in case, and pop a bit on the
wipe before use.

cookwitch

If you take some small plastic container like an old
Evian bottle, you can fill it with water and then rinse
your nether regions while sitting on the loo. Pat dry
with loo roll. Another trick is to take a couple of rags
or J-cloths, wet them in the washbasin and give
yourself a 'bath' in the toilet cubicle. Then you can
just throw the rag away and not have a stale flannel
making the tent whiffy! You'll be using plain water
with both methods, which shouldn't cause you any
problems.

silverfiligree

When I went to the Isle of Wight festival, I bought a
plant mister in Sainsbury's beforehand and filled it
with water. Every morning I'd do the wet-wipes-all-
over thing, then rinse my bits (I had to – just using the
wipes on their own would bring on thrush for me) by
spraying them afterwards. Pat dry with towel – job
done. It involved some awkward squatting positions
in the tent but hey, these things have to be done when
you're at a festival. I avoided the scary toilet cubicles,
though.

redshira

FACIAL CARE

I have not gone in for fancy facial care routines since I was a teenager, but lately I'm beginning to be mildly pissed off by the blackheads around my nose and on my chin. Has anyone any good facial care recommendations? Are those anti-blackhead scrub things any good? My current facial care consists of a brisk rub with a hot damp facecloth every morning, and moisturiser after showers (two to three times a week). I don't want anything much more complicated than that, nor anything that involves me spending a small fortune on products; I have more interesting things to do with my time and money than spend them on my face!

Bearing that in mind, suggestions ladies?

dorian

I found that washing my hands more often helped. I read the *Guardian* on the way to work and rubbing my face was creating more blackheads. These days I a) remind myself not to touch my face so much, and b) wash my hands more. It helps. Occasionally when the blackheads get the better of me I use Clearasil wipes before bed.

k425

The self-heating anti-blackhead treatment – I think it's Biore: it's in a green tube – worked very well for me as an occasional-use thing.

tamaranth

Origins do a charcoal mask (I think it's called 'Clean Sweep' or something similar) that is good.

sd

If you wash with a hot facecloth you're leaving your pores wide open. Rinse with cold water after washing to prevent as many blackheads.

ailbhe

QUICK FIX

I am going out tonight and I want to look 'nice'. Are there any 'instant fixes' I can try?

ec

Just splashing cold water on your face is better than nothing and can help a bit.

Cold used tea bags or cucumber slices on the eyes, a mask on the face (try one tablespoon of honey and one egg white mixed up).

Exfoliating body scrub for healthy skin: add sugar or salt to any body wash and rub in a circular motion everywhere.

tooth_fairy

Well, it depends how sadistic you're feeling, but a quick cold shower is the best way to brighten everything up – it gets your circulation going and brightens you up.

Salt in a little virgin olive oil makes a good face scrub if you haven't any already. Er, not too sure about eyes... chilled spoons held over/around them are supposed to be good at reducing redness and puffiness, but personally I'd recommend Benefit's 'Oh la lift' (not much use in this instance, but it's worth having some around in future).

madeleine

A long bath will help to relax you, and if you follow it with some gentle stretching exercises, and then make a mental effort to stand up straight with your shoulders back and down, that should help you not to feel hunched. It will also help to relax you mentally and emotionally! If you have any rose oil or rose-scented products, use them: rose is supposed to help put us in touch with our bodies, and it certainly makes me feel more glamorous and girly!

For your skin, do you have any natural (unflavoured) yoghurt in the house? Or any porridge oats? Either can form the basis of a nice face mask or scrub (oats are great for gentle exfoliation and moisturising; yoghurt is very cooling and soothing), to which you can add appropriate ingredients for your skin type: grated cucumber is good for oily or blemished skin, as are mashed strawberries. A bit of mashed banana or avocado is great for dry skin, as both are very moisturising and gentle.

Cold spoons, or cold used teabags (especially chamomile) or slices of cold cucumber over the eyes for 15 minutes should help to reduce redness or puffiness, and rinsing your face with cold water after washing off the remains of the face pack or scrub will tighten and brighten your skin a bit.

If you can spend a bit of time pampering yourself (slather on some nice scented body lotion, give yourself a mini manicure/pedicure, that sort of thing), you may find that helps you to feel a bit more glam too!

sushidog

I always found honey and yoghurt on the face a goodie (two tablespoons yoghurt, two tsp honey).

If you have it (and it's a long shot), two drops of undiluted rose absolute makes my skin glow even after a hard night, and it's pleasantly tingly...

Another good one is two egg whites spread on for five minutes.

laumiere

Exfoliation, moisturising, and drinking water and no alcohol.

The best exfoliator is by Dermologica. It's a rice-based thing, and I am swearing because I have just run out. Another good one is Lush, 'Little Japanese Girl', about £3.50. It moisturises at the same time. However, none of this is any good if you don't hydrate yourself. Drink at least two litres of water between now and then. Water, not fruit juice, or coffee, or alcohol. I should take my own advice.

juggzy

If I'm in a hurry, I wash with a hot hot hot facecloth, rub all over with it nearly dry to exfoliate, then rinse with cold water many many times. It works beautifully and I end up glowing with health and vigour. I find that I look more alert with my hair back away from my face, and standing up straight (roll shoulders up to ears and drop backwards) helps an awful lot too.

With more time, a proper bath or shower or even both – soaky bath first, washy shower after – and lots of lovely clean clean clothes and a proper hairbrush, taking ages and tipping my head up to get my whole scalp brushed. And teeth! – clean teeth make a big difference to me.

ailbhe

MOISTURISER

I need some help! For years I have been happily using Johnson's Baby Moisturising Cream on my face and it has been working really well for me. However, in the last couple of months it seems to have stopped working. My skin is so dry at the moment (I am guessing because of the cold weather mainly) and I am having to apply the moisturiser practically every 20 minutes because the dry skin just comes back so fast. Does anyone have any recommendations for a new moisturiser? One that actually works and really does combat dry skin in cold weather? Am at the end

of my tether as it's not a good look to have half your face falling off on a regular basis!

lostprophet

It's kinda pricey but Clinique Dramatically Different Moisturiser always works for me.

slappersire

I scrub the hell out of my face with a Clearasil pad then slap Palmers' on about 30 seconds later – does the job well.

redshira

You could try what I do – I put my normal moist-uriser on (St Ives daily moisturiser or similar), and then after about ten minutes I put some aqueous cream on over the top. It rubs in okay and is quite thick so doesn't dry out. As I put it on over my normal cream it doesn't make my skin too spotty. It doesn't smell very nice though!

af

You need to switch to something that contains oil, to stop the wind and cold from getting through. I'd suggest Lush stuff. I have 'Dream Cream' which is a big pot of 'body' moisturiser, but in weather like this when you needs something heavier than normal on your face (I use L'Oreal Lift on my face usually), it does a really good job without you having to pay through the nose. It's actually a lot cheaper than it appears because you need to use only a very small amount. Don't forget that Lush will happily do you a small pot, enough for a few uses, as a free sample if you ask for it. That way you can see if it's worth spending money on.

kissycat 1000

Try Nivea Soft – cheap and cheerful and very rich.

lm

Nivea/Lush Dream Cream. If you're feeling expensive, then Arden's '8 Hour Cream' works well too!

genie22

Bio-Oil is great (you can get it from Superdrug).

laumiere

Mine's a Boots Organics Day Shift one, and that seems to be doing the trick for me. I usually change moisturisers from summer to winter (usually from the Nivea SPF light on to the SPF-enriched one), but this seems to be OK year-round.

la bias

NAILS

For nails, I found the best thing to do was to eat avocado on a daily basis! My nails got noticeably stronger when I was doing this!

sushidog

SUNBURN

If you do get sunburnt what you really need is a good moisturiser (any will do), or aloe vera gel PLUS a few drops of peppermint oil. Mix the moisturiser in your hands with the peppermint oil and smooth it on. The mint will take the heat out of your skin and you'll feel like a new person!

pipistrellus

Lavender oil and aloe vera gel are good. If the burn is bad, avoid peppermint oil, as it will sting like obscenity of your choice.

ailbhe

Having grown up in a hot country, there was only one thing that soothed the myriad stinging sunburns I suffered as a child – calamine lotion.

il-maltija

No matter what you do, keep doing it. I mean, like every 20 minutes. Once it soaks into the skin, put more on. No, seriously. Keep it moist.

schmoomom

If the burn is radiating heat you'll be losing liquid from the inside too. Drink lots of water.

jj

You can take some aloe out of the bottle and mix it with some lavender and then slather on; if you use a miniature container you can keep it around for another go. Lavender is considered safe for most skin, but some people will react so do a sensitivity test first by putting a little of the mix on the inside of your elbow. The raw gel can be better than the bought stuff. I've a huge aloe plant myself.

wyvernfriend

DRY SKIN/ECZEMA

Just recently I've had a nasty outbreak of eczema on my face, thanks to the really cold and windy weather we've been having recently (oh yeah, and stress didn't help either!). Anyway, I moaned about this and my friend sent me a tube of Stellarium cream from Neal's Yard where she works. I've been using this product for literally two days and it has worked wonders. Most of the redness and sore dry patches have calmed down, and within a couple of days it should be pretty much cleared up.

missyk8

LASER HAIR REMOVAL

I recently had laser hair removal on my upper lip and between my eyebrows. Now the course is finished I thought I should update on how the whole thing went.

Overall, it was pretty ouchy, but each session was over very quickly (probably ten zaps in each place, the whole thing lasting two or three minutes in total) so nothing unbearable. For the upper lip, jamming your tongue as hard as you can up into the space between your teeth and your lip helps a lot. The middle of the upper lip is the most painful bit, so after the first session I had only the sides done, as I don't have much trouble with hair in the middle anyway.

I had six sessions. The day after the sixth session, the skin around my eyes puffed up horribly and stayed that way for three or four days. I don't have any proof that it was due to the laser, but the clinic were very unhelpful when I rang them about it, and there wasn't really anything else it could have been caused by. Once the swelling went down the bit between my eyebrows was tender and felt bruised for a few more days. My upper lip did not swell at all. I wonder whether the technician turned the laser up to a higher notch than usual, either because it was my last session or by mistake.

The effects have been OK but honestly not as good as I was expecting. My upper lip is better than it was, but I'm most disappointed with the eyebrows. I didn't realise beforehand, but the laser zaps a circular area with a diameter of 1 cm or so, so you don't get a clean line at the edges; as a result, although the middle bit of my eyebrows is now pretty much hair free, I'll still have to pluck the edges to get a clean line, which is a bit of a pain.

Overall, I don't think for me it was really worth the money (it is a pretty pricey treatment – I paid £200 for six treatments on the upper lip and £185 for six treatments on the area between the eyebrows). Obviously if you have more troublesome hair than I did, either over a larger area or in a more well-defined area, then it might still be worth it for you.

vicky l

LASER HAIR REMOVAL ADVICE

It is somewhat uncomfortable, but bearable. No major side effects that I've noticed (bar a bit of redness for a while). As to effectiveness, yes, definite effect. You will occasionally see electrolysis industry people claim that laser has never been proven to the standards that electrolysis has – and that appears to be true, but that doesn't mean it doesn't work.

Also, although you aren't supposed to wax/ pluck (because it destroys the path to the hair root that the laser needs to work), note you should be OK to trim/shave the offending hairs.

ab

HARD WATER

Before I moved to London five years
ago, I'd always lived in a soft water area.
When I first moved here I found washing
my hair in hard water really horrible. I was
told my hair (or I) would get used to it, but five
years on I still can't stand it. I never feel like my
hair is properly clean because it's still coated in
whatever is in the water, and I can't wash that
out. It makes my already dry frizzy hair feel
sticky, and at its worst I can't get a brush
through it properly. So, short of moving back up
north, does anyone have any suggestions what to
do to make my hair feel squeaky clean and
'normal' again?

dozle

There are two solutions. First, you need to get a hard
water testing kit (it's basically a piece of paper) and get
some bottled water and find one that is soft. Use that
to wash your hair in.

Alternatively, there is a hair product designed to
combat the effects of hard water. You can get it at
some hairdressers in the UK, but generally you have
to order it from the US as it isn't officially available
here. It comes with crystals which you rub on your
hair to take the calcium out of it. After your hair is
de-encrusted, both the colour and the feel of it will

improve. The brand is EC Mode (http://www.
malibu2000.com/content/Cn_Hair_Solutions_
Hard_Water.aspx).

siren

COLOURING HAIR

**Have many of you tried outrageous colours?
How have you got it done? What products? I
really would like to dye my (brown, long(ish))
hair neon red myself, but if the risk of damaging
fine hair is way too great please tell me so.**

tg

To go neon you would have to bleach it first, unless
you were blonde or unless you used those hairdresser
colours which bleach and lighten while simultane-
ously colouring your hair.

siren

Bleach bleach bleach, then dye. It's a terrible fuss, and
bad for your hair, but looks so good!

exploitedfairy

I have used 'Manic Panic' and also 'Midnight Madness' to make my hair purple, but I had to bleach my
light brown hair first.

The damage is real, but there are products such as conditioners to help with that.

ypau

I have fine but very strong hair and I've been bleaching/dying it for years (from dark brown originally) with no ill-effects. Red's a good colour to go for, as it has more staying power than a lot of other colours. I'd advise going to a hairdresser for the first time, especially if you've never dyed/bleached before – it can be quite worrying feeling the heat that comes off a bleaching head for the first time – going to a pro's just a bit more reassuring with things like that. Then, you can do the re-dyeing yourself when the colour starts to fade. Added tip for hair-dyeing: don't use the crappy gloves that come with dye-packets (depending on what type of dye you use) – get latex gloves from the chemist. *So* much easier to work with.

cm

I dunno about outrageous, but my hair is various shades of blue/purple (depending on how recently I dyed it; at the moment some of the bluer bits have faded to a rather fetching turquoise, and the rest is more blue than purple, but sort of streaky). It doesn't look very outrageous, because it's dead straight and cut in a fairly simple style (an asymmetric bob).

I do it myself; every four or five months I bleach it (I'm fortunate in that it bleaches fairly easily, without getting too damaged), and then I dye it every three weeks or so using La Riche Directions; I use Midnight Blue and Dark Plum, making some wide streaks with each and then mixing some of both together and using that on the rest of my hair. I then put on a (very sexy) shower cap, put a towel over my pillow, and sleep with the dye on. (It's vegetable-based and doesn't contain any bleach or ammonia or other nasty chemicals, so this doesn't damage my hair). I wash it off the next morning in the shower.

If you're thinking of doing your hair, please do a strand test first, so that if it does damage your hair, or goes wrong, or you just don't like it, you're not committed. Get some professional advice, even if you decide to dye at home. Also, bear in mind that strong, unnatural colours often don't last very well, so you may find yourself 'topping up' the colour more fre-quently than with a plain brown or whatever.

sushidog

Mine's blue as well; and I do the same thing with leaving it on overnight (though with clingfilm rather than shower cap!). I've recently started using Special Effects (available online from http://www.haircrazy.-com) which I find lasts much longer than Directions.

jk

DRY HAIR

Dear Ladies, I have currently got hopelessly dry hair, despite all the extra-nourishing conditioners and potions I have been throwing at it. Suspect

the winter has killed it good'n proper, but I don't want to cut it off as it has taken me ages to grow!

Does Pantene 'Winter Rescue' work?! I'm getting marginally desperate.

easternpromise

Frizz Ease deep conditioner is really good; they also have a really really light spray-on conditioner which should keep it protected against the weather and stuff. I swear by Frizz Ease though.

kaz_pixie

Coconut oil, mayonnaise and honey makes an excellent hair masque. Try it with clingfilm one day – and wash it off in the evening.

genie22

Two suggestions:

- Henna seems to help the condition of a lot of people's hair.
- Oil. Coconut oil is good but any oil will work – try an Indian grocery for hair oil. Either comb a small amount through your hair and just leave it till you next wash it (very small amount) or put lots in, leave for a few hours/overnight and wash out.

sk

I love Aussie Miracle Hair 3 Minute Repair. Super!

feath

RINGLETS?

Has anyone got any bright ideas about how I can get my long, somewhat frizzy, hair to go into sleek tight ringlets for at least a few hours? Any suggestions about the best way to curl it and how to get it to hold there for a while?

dozle

How I get it to work in my VERY curly hair: wash it and condition heavily; towel dry and then straighten (either wet-to-dry straighteners or blow-dry/straighteners) – using heat protection spray to keep it sleek and tidy.

Once all of your hair is sleek and straight, tong it or put in heated rollers. While this seems like a long way for a shortcut, it does work beautifully – at least on my hair – and is the only way to guarantee curls without frizz. If your hair is naturally curly it will take the curls (tongs or rollers) quite quickly. And use lots of hairspray on the curls.

td

HAIR – SUNSCREEN RECOMMEN-DATIONS?

Aargh! In the last week I've been out in the beautiful sunshine and my hair has gone all crispy! The split ends were nipped off the other night, but it still feels like stroking a coconut. Any suggestions? I've used Lush henna con-ditioner on it and given it a good soak with Aussie Hair Miracle, which has improved the condition but not much. It tends to burn then get better as I condition it. What I'm looking for is a sunscreen to stop it getting in this state. Ideally I'm after something veggie that doesn't smell of horrible chemicals. Thanks!

jj

Before you go out smooth Lush's The Strokes through it. Acts as a hair sunscreen.

laumiere

I often use Boots Coconut and Almond Oil leave-in conditioner, which is a spray for dry hair (tag: 'Moisturises hair for softness and shine'). It smells of coconut (surprisingly enough) and I use it as a detangler. It's cheap and nice. I can't speak for its veggie-ness, and the ingredients list is full of unpronounceable chemicals, but I like it.

lfk

Go to a Afro-Caribbean hair shop if you can and buy a product from them for damaged hair. They do huge amounts of stuff for just this type of damage.

cookwitch

Well, I swear by Phytologie products to get hair back to peak condition. They also make an excellent sunscreen that will prevent further damage.

lm

HENNA AND DYE

In a vain attempt to keep my hair a nice bright red while in decent enough condition not to crack and fall out in my hands, I've reluctantly decided to go back to using henna. (Leaves your hair in much better condition, but colour fades more quickly and you get a kind of 'henna halo' in the sunlight.) Hair is shoulder length but dry and porous despite using decent conditioner all the time. Anyway: you're not supposed to use

henna on top of hair dye. It would take me about two years to grow out all the dye in my hair and I'm not prepared to have my mousy faded red roots plus white bits on show for two weeks, never mind all that time. Can you really, really not use henna on top of dye? What's the worst that could happen? And if I really can't, what could I do instead?

99

I don't see why not. Maybe do a test strand, a small swatch, and see what happens.

feath

I henna my hair – Body Shop's raging red is the best colour for me. I bleach the strips then henna over the top of that. Meant to be a big no-no, but in over three years I've never had any problems, and I like the way it comes out. I always use the same henna and the same blonding stuff (a 'gentle' highlighting bleach, rather than pure peroxide) though – I'm not risking changing anything.

But your hair could go green or some other bad colour. The worst-case scenario is that the henna and the chemical dye will react badly and burn your hair... but that's rare. The best way to find out is to take a sample of hair from your hairbrush, henna it, and see what happens.

And if you do go the henna route, can I recommend:

- Wrap your hair in clingfilm, and use a hairdryer on it at regular intervals to keep it hot. The hotter the henna is, the redder your hair will go.

Massage your head to squidge it round under the clingfilm while it's hot too. I've never found adding wine or cloves of coffee or lemon or anything else made as much difference as heat (although I still add cloves and cinnamon to make it smell better!).

- Boots Organics Henna Conditioner. It comes with a warning that it will stain tiles and towels. It's red. Very good for keeping colour in your hair. Don't bother with the matching shampoo unless you really want to though, it makes little difference.

silke

I'd say do the strand test and see; bear in mind that adding red wine to henna will tone down the orangey-ness in favour of red (as you'd expect, really!), and coffee will give it a browner sheen; might be worth experimenting a bit.

sushidog

I've done it recently (dyed with henna over bleached and dyed highlights) without any problems! I did do a strand test first, though. (FWIW, bleach and dye were about three months old when I used henna.)

yanata

I henna over dye and haven't had any trouble, I use the same henna as Silke and love it. Just about to try the red wine, cloves and cinnamon route as well. Seems like an awful waste of red wine though...

nb

DANDRUFF

One of my poor teenagers is plagued by dandruff at present. I know it's a hormonal thing and will settle down eventually, but he really is suffering a snowstorm right now. Head and Shoulders is not working – any suggestions, either dietary or topical?

mendi

Tea Tree shampoo (a cheap supermarket one is fine) used regularly should help. And depending on hair length, a Tea Tree conditioner is good too. I used to use the Paul Mitchell one, which is lovely, but it's about £6 or so a bottle.

mmcpoland

My son is 13 and has the same problem. I bought him the 'hybrid' shampoo bar from Lush when the Head and Shoulders stopped working, and it does seem to work. I find I have to make sure he's washing it all out properly, though (that's *any* shampoo, not just the Lush one) because he doesn't, as a rule, and not washing it out properly does seem to make a big difference.

My mother bought him Dry Scalp Intensive Lotion (Boots own brand) but I wasn't convinced by it, so don't waste your money. We have also used T-Gel, but again with limited success.

ee

Don't use Head and Shoulders, it's bad. It *gives* me dandruff!

Perhaps shampoos without sodium laureth sulphate in them may help. It may be an urban myth, but apparently it's a very harsh foaming agent.

Thursday Plantation Tea Tree Shampoo is ace.

kg

I loathe Head and Shoulders with a passion – it just used to make my head sore. I find Nizoral works best (or Boots own version), and then once it's under control, alternating between that and a nice Tea Tree shampoo from Superdrug. The Timotei anti-dandruff was brilliant, but I have trouble finding that these days.

What I find triggers mine is stress (I had my first big flare-up during my GCSEs) and my head getting too hot, so it's worse at the height of summer, or when it's really cold so we have the central heating on most of the time. Double-bagging the pillows and changing the top cover twice as often, and washing them and the towel he uses to dry his hair in a slightly hotter wash is supposed to help kill off the yeast that exacerbates the problem.

aligoestonz

Household

ONION AND GARLIC SMELLS

After you've chopped onions or garlic rub your hands with used coffee grounds – it gets rid of the smell better than soap can.

alt

OPENING JARS

To open a jar when the lid is being an arse, tap it on a hard surface first – it breaks the seal and makes it a doddle to open. No jar of jam gets the better of me now.

alt

Wear marigold gloves when opening jars: it gives you super strength!

df

OIL STAINS

Use clarifying shampoo to get oil stains or car grease out of clothes.

boneist

BLOCKED DRAINS

Does anyone have any magic tips for clearing a blocked drain? Our early 1960s plumbing has been draining the bath slowly for a long time. I plunge regularly and use a hair trap in the plug hole, but recently it has got a lot worse. If you take a shower or wash your hair you are left with several inches of water in the bath that then take ages to drain away. A bath takes about an hour.

Loath though I am to resort to evil chemicals I have used Harpic Power Jet (an expensive waste of time) and Mr Muscle 2 Liquid Foamer. The latter eased the problem a little. It's very difficult to get under our bath and I'm a bit scared to try and start undoing things that I might not be able to get back together. Paying for a plumber is out of the question for the foreseeable future.

zoefruitcake

It depends what's blocking it, but it might be worth buying a bottle of Veet (or whatever they're calling it now; hair removal cream, anyway), pouring that down, and leaving it for a while before rinsing. If the blockage is composed partly or principally of hair, that should help.

Caustic soda is another option; it's foul stuff, and you'll need to open all the windows and get out of the bathroom as soon as you've done the business, and stay out for a while, but you may find that it helps, and it's cheaper than a lot of the 'labelled' options.

sushidog

You can buy bendy things at DIY stores for pushing clogs out of a drain. They're called 'plumber's mates', they're long flexible metal rods (they look a bit like thin shower hoses), and the idea is that you just shove it down the drain and hopefully push the clog out. If I recall correctly, one will cost you about £5–10. Trouble, is they're no good unless the clog is within 6 ft of your plughole. I once had a blocked sink and thought the clog was within the first few feet of pipe. It turned out to be on the other side of the kitchen, and required a plumber in the end.

lozette

NEW PAINT

To get rid of the smell of new paint put half a cut onion in the room. Works a treat

chewbeaker

PET
INSURANCE

Anyone able to recommend a good pet insurer? I've got two cats, both neutered females, Freya is 6, Aubrey is 3. Am currently getting bogged down by policies! Any help gratefully received!

jules

Our cat's with Petplan, as recommended by hubby the vet.

vf

PetPlan. Never had any trouble with them, they pay out promptly and the forms are simple to complete!

k425

Another vote here for PetPlan – they've paid out about double what I've paid them in premiums for my cat over eight years, never quibbled over a claim, and the cheque has always arrived within 10 days of the form going in.

cazmanian minx

THERMOS FLASK SMELLS

I've got a lovely thermos flask, but it smells! I wash it thoroughly after each use, and I soak it too, but it smells of old soup still. Is there anything I can do to get rid of this? Because it's making tea and coffee taste funny too.

*_mardybum_*

Use sterilising fluid – the stuff people use for sterilising babies' bottles.

pb

Milton, or false teeth cleaning tablets. I used to use those for the teapot and they work a treat.

k425

First, clean with half a lemon, then sprinkle some baking soda in and let that dry completely before washing it out. Also ensure the flask gets to dry out completely at least every second day, rather than being refilled all the time and staying damp/having fluid in it.

silja

OILY HANDS

Washing up liquid and sugar works better than
Swarfega for when you've been messing with
your car engine and you've got oily hands.

alt

DISH-
WASHERS

I am lucky enough to live in rented
accommodation that comes with a dishwasher. I
don't use it much, because I can't seem to get it
to get my stuff clean enough. I don't put really
dirty pans in or anything, and I always rinse
plates etc. first. What I find is gritty residue on
things, on the surface of plates and even up
inside glasses that have been on the shelf upside
down. I put the recommended amount of Finish
liquid in, and I also use rinse aid when it needs it,
and I don't overfill the thing either. And the salt
levels appear to be correct.

So, ladies of the loos, how do I get it to do its
job properly?

kg

The amount of salt you need depends on whether you are in a hard or soft water area. On mine there's a little pointer that you can move around, depending on the hardness of your water, so although it may think it has enough salt that might be misleading for the area that you are in. Also, this page might help: http://www.dishwasher-care.org.uk/trouble.html.

aligoestonz

Make sure you get all the excess crap off the plates before you put them in – a mushroom swishing around can make a difference.

If the stuff is sitting in the dishwasher a while before you get to washing, run a water-only wash over it, as a prewash, to soften food debris. Keep the filters clear. Check that the water coming in is fine. Check the salt levels. Use a decent detergent and rinse aid. Try those three- in-one tablets, even though they are expensive. Load it up properly. Don't overload – better to do two washes than have to do the same wash again and again to remove debris.

Clean the dishwasher regularly, and hang a dish-washer freshener up to keep it smelling nice.

vf

SILK STAINS

If you have water stains on silk try steaming the stain over a kettle and then rub the sheeny side of the silk with another clean bit of the silk. Somehow it lifts the mark out (it's also good for getting the honk out of vintage dresses).

jackie

RENTING FROM A LETTING AGENT

You can get references from a temp agency, though it helps if you've been with one or two for a period of time and you have payslips or bank statements saying you've got a reasonably steady income – enough to pay the rent.

Letting agents are simple enough – visit as many as you can in the area you are looking at. Make sure you have a clear idea of what you are looking for and how much you want to pay, so you don't waste time looking at unsuitable places. Take a friend with you to view potential places if you can, for a second opinion.

dozle

My husband and I have just moved and had no end of hell, because he has a temp contract – although he has been working in the same place for four years. Luckily a good friend stood as a guarantor, so it got sorted out – but be careful if you're still temping. Some places are way too strict. So really, just be careful which agent you go with – some are stricter than others.

suv

I've been living alone for a little while now, and I have to say, it's much better than having housemates, so good luck with it!

Some tips: make a list of what you want in a flat. Are you OK with a shower and no bath, or do you need a bath? How big a space are you looking for? Furnished or unfurnished? Check out ads in the paper, to get an idea of what sort of prices you should be expecting to pay in different areas. When you go and see the agents, or talk to them on the phone, ask them lots of questions: When do they check your references? When can you expect to hear back from them? Do they have a minimum length for contracts? What happens about any maintenance work that needs doing? Is there an emergency number in case your plumbing springs a leak over the weekend? What happens if you need to cut your lease short for some reason?

Read the contract before you sign anything. I know it's dull, but you need to know whose responsibility it is to fix things and how quickly they will undertake to do stuff, and so on. A while ago my drains got blocked and it took over a week to get them cleared (during which time I had raw sewage backing up into my plumbing), and then they tried to charge me for it, thanks to some odd phrasing in the contract, so it really is worth checking! They sometimes also try to tack on all sorts of extra charges, which you can query if you haven't signed the contract, but once it's signed they can just shrug and say 'It's in the contract'.

Also, bear in mind that the prices are sometimes flexible, so it is OK to put in a slightly lower offer; I did that on my current place, and ended up paying £50 a month less than was being asked. You can also bargain a bit: my landlord wanted me to sign a year's lease rather than the normal six months, so I said I'd do that if he'd install a washing machine, rather than me having to rent one.

sushidog

My biggest bit of advice, from five years of renting houses, is to make sure you get an inventory, and make sure you check it. Every letting agent I've ever had has tried to screw money out of us at the end of the tenancy by claiming we'd damaged the property, or that things that had never been there in the first place were missing, or similar. Letting agencies are mostly quite nice at the beginning of the tenancy, but in my experience they all turn into gits at the end when you're trying to leave and get your deposit back.

ej

Photographs are also good – before you move in and when you're moving out. Preferably digital or date stamped. Our old landlady has charged us £40 for not taking down some shelves that were there when we moved in! Luckily we did have a digital photo of them.

kiss_me_quick

BEANS

If you cook dried beans do not add salt or they will never soften, and if you add bicarb they won't cause you to be so gassy afterwards.

cookwitch

WASHING JEANS

I've got some of the dark arts of womanhood sorted (handwashing bras, being quite good at plucking my eyebrows, always knowing where my boyfriend's shoes are...) but there's one thing I still don't know how to do...

How do you stop jeans getting swirly patterns and lines on them? I like quite dark blue jeans, and after even a few washes the dye starts to look uneven. Crinkle marks and creases stay visible in the colour even after ironing, and in extreme cases it starts to look like I've deliberately done some kind of tie-dye effect. Is there a way to stop this happening?

tb

I wash my jeans inside out, that seems to help with the creases. Also, if dye is coming out, maybe you're washing them at too high a temperature? I only ever wash at 30–40 degrees, and my black jeans are still in pretty reasonable nick.

silke

What everyone else said – but also I add half a handful of salt to really over-dyed items, which helps them not to fade/run too much.

batswing

MOVING HOUSE?

If you take stuff to the local waste tip/recycling centre, it's worth looking to see if anyone's been throwing out decent strong cardboard boxes. I took a load of junk down there and discovered a big container full of flattened cardboard boxes. Grabbed the closest decent-condition and strong ones (look for double-walled boxes), and hey presto, I have three great boxes more to pack, completely free.

I'm guessing, since it's a recycling centre, that they wouldn't care if recycling actually meant someone wandering away with boxes to reuse them – they certainly didn't stop me, though I did get a couple of 'what is she doing walking that way with the boxes' looks.

I may well be back for some more one lunchtime when I take some more junk down there. I figure that works out well – I give them some junk and take away some unwanted cardboard boxes instead. Swapsies. So there you go.

Free boxes to be had at the local tip/recycling centre. Why bother paying £50–100 for a pack of brand-new 'I'm moving home' boxes, when you can get them free?

velvetpurrs

CURTAINS

How do I hang curtain wires for my net curtains? I have wire but it's in one really long length and needs to be cut into four for four windows. What do I cut it with and do I make it slightly shorter than the width between the hooks on the window frame so it's under tension from being stretched?

urp

I used my kitchen scissors to cut the wires. I also made them a tiny bit shorter that the width after my first attempt made them too short and the wire pulled out of the hooks. It's always easier to trim a little more off.

kate atkin-wright

It's best to go conservatively – when it stretches, as it eventually does, you can always trim it again a bit more. Re: cutting – wire cutters are best, just don't use any scissors you wouldn't want to spoil because it can damage the blades (if I had kitchen scissors I loved I'd be inclined to buy some cheap pincers with a wire-cutting bit on them instead).

antigone76

CLEANING WITH ESSENTIAL OIL

Sweet orange essential oil (which is as cheap as chips, especially if you buy it in 100 ml bottles) is *fabulous* for cleaning stuff – especially the top of the cooker.

alt

CLEANING SHOWER CURTAINS

We've got a manky shower curtain at the flat which has mouldy stuff all over it, and I don't know how to get it clean. Or indeed if it should simply be chucked out and replaced – but apparently one of the previous housemates had a miracle solution to it that used to get it clean again. What needs to be done? It's a pretty basic, plastic curtain.

starmix

Bleach should do it. Leave it soaking in a bleach/
water solution overnight.

cookwitch

Stick it in the washer with some old white towels and
some oxy bleach (e.g. Ace), and wash on a cool cycle.

gemma

You can get anti-mould sprays which are quite good;
spray on, leave for half an hour or longer, rinse off.

sushidog

When mine was last manky I washed it (left it to soak
in the bath) with some bio washing detergent and a
spot of oxy bleach. It was a miracle cure.

classytart

Soak in Milton solution for an hour and stick in a 30
degree wash.

laumiere

GOLDFISH

Ailing goldfish may be revived by being placed
in cold water for an hour!

kimkali

LADY OF THE FLIES

Recently, we've discovered that during storms, night-time, rain, fog etcetera, hordes of flies are sheltering in our (shut) windows, in the crack of the hinge between the window and the frame bit. I have no idea how they get in there even! So when we open windows, huge nasty buzzy flies come in. Does this happen to anyone else? Is there any way to stop it? It's so horrible...

bee

I hate them too. I have a big skylight window in my kitchen, they fly in through the open door and up to it to try and get out again. They must be pretty dense. Anyway, you could try dabbing some citronella oil in your window crack or get a sticky fly paper – not a pretty sight when it's full, but a great sense of revenge.

aellia

First, lighting candles and incense around the place helps. They don't like that.

Second, I found a clever little device in Robert Dyas. It's about two inches high, is made of plastic and hangs from a hook on the wall. It looks a bit like one of those air freshener things. Anyway, since I hung it up we've had far fewer flies, so I think it works. And it doesn't smell like the sprays do...

starmix

They are cluster flies (Google provides some info on them and some things to try, too). You may need to get pest control in to deal with them, but at the end of the day I think they are very hard to get rid of, so it might take a few attempts.

velvetpurrs

CLEANING WINDOWS

When cleaning windows use newspaper to get the water off and leave a smear/streak-free shine. Vinegar makes windows sparkle too, but it also makes them smell.

silvernik

HOW OFTEN DO YOU WASH YOUR BED LINEN?

Every week. If I do it every Sunday I remember, and if I don't, I forget. The mattress protector gets done every fortnight, on the 'did we do that last week?' principle.

I grew up thinking that weekly was normal and we were terrible slobs for doing it less often. At one stage I was washing bedding less often than monthly.

ailbhe

I was conditioned by mum to change it every week, but lately that has slipped to about once a fortnight. I don't think I could leave it any longer than that – I hate the feeling when it starts to get a bit grubby.

phoenix 1979

When it needs it, which can be after a few days or several weeks. If I'm being busy and it's only getting crawled into for about five hours on only half the nights in the week, not much point. If my other half is visiting and, well, it's seeing a lot of use, rather more often.

I have two thin duvets each with a separate cover,

so while one has its cover in the wash it sits on top. Effectively still a thick duvet and the one next to me is still covered.

shermarama

Every two weeks. Unless the cat has vomited on it, of course.

juggzy

Every week, to kill off the dust mites (I'm allergic), and a duvet cover change and wash every couple of weeks too. Duvet/pillows wash every two to three months... and of course, don't forget to vacuum the mattress, as that gets a lot of the mites out of your bedding... bleugh! Oh and the undersheet thingie too. Very hot wash.

siv

REMOVING WALLPAPER

To strip even the toughest wallpaper don't bother with a steamer: simply knock up a bucket of wallpaper paste, brush on liberally and leave to soak for an hour or so. The wallpaper will then fall off back to the plaster when you get the scraper to it. If it doesn't, leave to soak for a while longer.

paulie

CAT TOYS

Best-value cat toys ever have to
be Culpepers' catnip toys – pure
enjoyment for them, amusement at
stoned kitties for me!

bee

I'll second stuffed catnip toys. I get the ones that look
like sticks of dynamite because they seem to last much
longer. We've got one that's been going about a year
now – she throws it at me!

cookwitch

Thirded – mine's catnip-stuffed vet (really) is only a
bit tatty after a year. They tend to pass out all boggly-
eyed in a drug-induced haze before the toy gets
wrecked!

JZ

A ping-pong ball and a catnip mouse go a long way in
most households!

k425

Ours have a Cat Spa, you get them from Pet City for about £10. All you need to do is put catnip on it and away they go.

am

CAT URINE

The best stuff to get rid of cat urine is something called Pet Fresh by Urine Off. (www.petfresh.co.uk) It just saved our carpet.

cookwitch

Cat pee can be cleaned up with cheap vodka – the alcohol breaks down either the proteins or the fats (can't remember which) that cause the smell. A few drops of sweet orange essential oil in with it will stop your cat going near again.

alt

IRONING

Who irons? I ask because I don't iron anything, ever. Literally, I can't remember when I last ironed something – I'm terrible at it anyway,

and it's never seemed worth it. Which slightly horrifies my mum.

When my daughter starts going to school I suppose I'll have to iron her uniform, but at the moment ironing just doesn't seem necessary. Most clothes don't crumple too badly and lots of creases fall out when you put clothes on. But am I just being slovenly?

yh

We never iron! Our ironing board is gathering dust in the corner of our spare bedroom at the moment, and I honestly do not know where our iron is. I think I ironed my blouse before my graduation, but I don't bother ironing anything else. I honestly don't see the point unless it's a smart shirt or something and it has lots of creases. I'm not going to waste time and electricity doing something I don't feel is necessary, and I don't feel slovenly about it either. Neither should you!

bonnie

I don't iron, heck I don't even own an iron. If something is creased, I'll hang it up in the bathroom with me while I have a hot shower, seems to do the trick. Anything like suits that really do need ironing get dry cleaned.

liese

I iron most clothes (but not underwear or sheets or pyjamas) unless they are made of sweat pant material. I hate seeing people in unironed clothes.

mendi

Life's too short to stuff a mushroom – or operate an iron! Yesterday I ironed a few shirts, but only because they had come out of a box following our move and they looked like it. Normally I have one item of clothing that requires ironing (a white linen shirt), and I iron it just before I put it on.

morganalefay

I don't iron anything. I hang clothes on hangers when wet, and might iron something that is really bad about once or twice a year.

In my little atlas I have on my desk I have something I cut out of a magazine in September 1999 and I used to have stuck on my computer at work. When people used to ask me how I had time to read so many books I'd ask them if they ironed. If they said yes I'd point them to the cutting, which states:

THE AVERAGE WOMAN SPENDS 117
HOURS A YEAR IRONING
(SOURCE: LENOR)

My mother even irons her dusting rags.

zoefruitcake

I am the only one who does always iron!? I'd love to not be able to iron, but I don't like messy wrinkly clothes. I tried not ironing once, but we all looked a mess!

How do you all do it? Do you have to take the clothes out of the machine as soon as it finishes, then shake the wrinkles out of them or something?

The only things I don't iron are pants, socks etc.

rebecca mcallister

One of my friends' kids came home from a friend's house and reported with excitement that they had a surfboard in their kitchen cupboard. It took ages for my friend to work out that the other family had an ironing board.

k425

My mum used to be a school nurse and likes things ironed properly. I never really bothered with ironing until I moved home for a year, and Mum ironed my clothes – I now iron everything, and do my boyfriend's ironing too – he's quite happy for it not to be done!

I'm aware I'm in the minority though – I don't know any of my friends who iron if they can help it!

nikki

I iron clothes when they look like they need it, so most natural fabrics get at least a quick ironing. I sometimes skip ironing casual clothes, but work clothes always get done. I also have a peculiar habit of ironing clothes into a different shape – I have lots of cardigans which I stretch when I iron them to make the sleeves longer.

I don't wear jeans very often any more, but I used to iron them to make them softer before wearing them because I didn't like how they were hard when clean, even if I used lots of fabric softener. Also sewing: it's impossible to make seams without the use of an iron.

I think I must be one of the people who are pushing the average number of ironing hours up.

silverclear

I don't do it unless I want to wear something and it's creased. The boy does his own if it needs it. I do actually quite like ironing, though. I used to work for a domestic cleaning company and I also ironed for them, because I got paid extra to do it.

ba

FLEAS IN THE HOUSE

Start by vacuuming, and go to professional extermination quickly. When we had no pets at all we once came home from a two-week holiday to find that the few fleas that had been in the house before we left had responded to the lack of food by BREEDING. I still have the scars on my shins.

We found professional extermination cost not much more than a tin of totally ineffective flea spray from the shop, and it actually worked, which helps a lot.

ailbhe

BEDS

I made the mistake earlier this year of buying a cheap mattress when we bought our new bedstead. It is awful and I have problems getting restful sleep anyway, and so this horrid thing has to go.

We have a 5 ft bedstead and just need a mattress, not a divan. We are also quite big, so the mattress needs to be able to survive a bit of rough and tumble through normal use, let alone the more interesting stuff...

We are going to bounce around a few at bed stores, but would like to know if there is a trend out there where certain brands are better than others – i.e. you have found the perfect make!

Any help appreciated.

pumpkin

I love the mattress I got from Ikea (so much so that when we got rid of the Ikea bed we kept the mattress for our proper bed). They do a range of different hardnesses and stuff, and I found them very helpful.

jinn

My mum just got a new one and it is the best thing I've ever laid on! It was from the Co-op and has a latex layer on the top; it keeps you really warm and is wonderful to lie on. It was pricey though, at £400.

rebecca mcallister

I can HIGHLY recommend the Sealy Posturepedic mattresses.

cookwitch

I have the best mattress in the world, and as mattresses go it was on the cheap side. Made by Relaxan, firm as anything (although they do different firmnesses for preference – I like mine solid) – it's a foam mattress, *really* holds its shape, and has no springs to poke into places you don't want springs poking into. The land-lady bought it, but I *think* it was around the £120 mark – the man, who's slept on it, thought it'd be around £300 minimum it's so good.

cm

Hubby and I love our Dunlopillo mattress.

kate atkin-wright

BOBBLY CLOTHES

There is no need to buy de-bobblers to rejuvenate sweatshirts, duffel coats or felt – just shave them with a disposable razor.

muggsy

PILLOWS

My husband's (feather) pillow... well, it stinks. A year ago I threw out his last one because frankly it smelt of fungus, and this one is going the same way. It says on it that you shouldn't wash it. I suspect I shouldn't try, as the feathers will clump. However, there has to be SOMETHING I can do to clean it up, without wrecking it, or buying a new one?

suzylou

I have washed feather pillows successfully before now. Do it on the delicates programme, and for drying you need somewhere that you can lie it flat but not a solid surface – draped over a clotheshorse would do, or I laid mine on my rotary clothesline. Shake it up every so often while it's drying (takes a couple of days), and it should end up fine.

dorian

To save the trouble of cleaning in future, buy a pillow protector, like a mattress protector-cum-extra pillow-case, that you can zip the pillow inside and remove at any time to clean.

smallblakflower

CAT HAIR

A damp rubber glove is the best thing for removing cat fur/hair from clothing and furnishings. Just brush your hand over whatever is hairy and then rinse it off. Reusable and effective.

am

LAUNDRY HELP!

How do I turn my lovely white bed linen white again???

cazmanian minx

Variously: oxyclean in the wash, boil wash, line drying in the sunshine (though that might be difficult at certain times of year).

myf

Soak your linen in a cold bleach solution for an hour or so. Rinse, and then wash on the boil wash. If it's still yellowish, repeat this procedure, and add a dose of

Vanish powder to the washing powder on the boil wash.

Once you've got your linen white again, you can keep it that way by regular boil-washing and use of Vanish with the washing powder. (Vanish is wonderful stuff, and also does a great job of removing grime from shirt-collars.)

dorian

DRY CLEANING AND AVOIDING IF POSSIBLE

I bought a coat for my daughter this morning; got it home and realised it's dry-clean only. The label states that it's 35% polyester, 35% acrylic, 25% wool, 5% other fibres, so I'm presuming that dry cleaning is advised because of the wool content. If that's the case it should be safe to machine wash on a cold cycle, but I'm not sure and was hoping that some of you nice ladies might be able to help me out. Has anyone had any similar experience and managed to machine wash without any problems, or got any cunning

**alternatives – ignoring the obvious of being a
sensible mother and buying practical clothes?**

madeleine

I've machine washed my dry-clean coats and they've
been fine, but I am far from a laundry expert so I'd wait
and see what other more knowledgeable people say first.

I keep buying things and then realising that they're
totally impractical as well. Drives me mad!

seren

That's been my experience. Dry cleaning doesn't exist
in my reality apart from for seriously expensive suits. I
generally ecowash on 40 degrees and have only ever
had one 'I really should have dry cleaned that' disaster
– which was stretchy suit trousers, go figure.

lisa g

STICKY STUFF ON WALLS

If you have glue from stickers or sticky tape on
your wall or any painted surface you can use
firelighter fluid to remove with a piece of
cotton wool. This actually works for most types
of adhesive. If really stubborn, try isopropyl
alcohol -ask your chemist for 'rubbing alcohol'.

paulie

LAMINATE FLOORING

I am soon to move house and my new living room has laminate flooring. Have any of you got any good tips on how to clean it? I've seen a few cleaning products while browsing in Asda and some said not to use on flooring as it might cause you to slip and slide, which isn't a great idea when you're as clumsy as I am and have a two-year-old. So any of you with laminate flooring, apart from sweeping up any bits off it, how do you clean it?

julie

You can actually get laminate floor cleaner. I know you can buy it from places like Bettaware and Kleeneze. Oh, and here: http://www.completelyflooring.co.uk.

cookwitch

I use one of those Swiffer thingies that has wet cloths and dry ones. Mostly I just go over any nasty patches (yay for cats with frequent hairballs) with the wet one and follow with the dry one so there's no slipperiness. For a general sweep around I use my spiffy new anti-pet-hair Hoover and the dry Swiffer cloth for the unhooverable bits.

hs

Mop, warm water, and multisurface cleaner (I'd recommend Ecover, for environmental reasons, and it seems to do the trick quite happily).

jk

Get a cloth, sit a cat on the cloth, play cat-curling.

cm

I Dyson up the fluff and then just mop it once a week (our downstairs hallway is laminate). I do Dyson it practically every day to pick up cat hair and rug fluff, though.

anna

Hoover and occasional mop (the J-cloth-on-a-pad style mop – on a flat surface you don't need something as hefty as the old-fashioned string mops, they make the floor far too wet!). I tend to use hot water to speed up how fast it dries.

sea_of_flame

KITCHEN SMELLS

A small bowl of bicarbonate of soda in the fridge will completely neutralise any lingering smells. Likewise, sprinkle a dessertspoon of bicarb in the bottom of the kitchen bin before you put the bin bag in. No smells.

moggy

MOULD AND DAMP

I have just pulled my two corsets out of the tallboy and they are covered with mould! I'm currently living in a downstairs flat, with no ventilation (nothing over the windows, or in the bathroom), and we are really suffering from condensation. Any tips on how I can prevent this from happening? Leaving a window open isn't really an option (as we have no central heating either!).

jules

You can get mini dehumidifiers (intended for use in cupboards) pretty reasonably at Argos.

lozette

Unfortunately condensation can only be sorted out by heating the building so the walls/windows are warm, and by ventilating so the damp air can be replaced by drier air. Remove all sources of moisture – that means having a window open after a bath/shower, opening a window when cooking (keeping the door to bathroom/kitchen shut to keep the moisture-laden air confined to that room only while bathing/cooking), and not drying clothes by hanging them up indoors – hang them outside, or tumble dry (but put that vent hose out the window).

Any form of heating is going to help – electric radiators/fan heaters etc. – but the key to stopping condensation is steady heat. Warm air holds more moisture than cold air. You cook/have a bath/exhale overnight, and that's warm air, with lots of moisture in. This meets a cold surface, and the moisture condenses out on to it. Make that surface warmer and it won't condense out as much, but by far the best solution is to get rid of the damp air to the outside before it finds the colder surfaces.

Heating a place part of the day and letting it cool the rest of the time can make condensation worse – again, when it's warm the air holds a lot more water, and as the place cools it condenses on to everything it can find. Low-level but continuous heat can be better than short stints of higher heat if the intervening periods allow the building to cool down too much.

Keeping clothes dry: I would suggest getting some plastic boxes that seal well, and getting some silica gel sachets (often to be found packed with laptops/camera gear etc., but can be bought without resorting to expensive gadget purchases!) to throw in with them. The silica gel will absorb any damp, and as long as the boxes are kept sealed the clothes should remain mould free.

velvetpurrs

MOTIVATION

I really need some motivation to keep our house clean and tidy. I have recently had a baby, and even though we have a cleaner once a week the house is trashed again by the next day. I used to use FLYlady (www.flylady.net) and that's excellent, but my motivation for all that is zilch.

My mother in law is coming to stay and even that doesn't motivate me. HELP!!!

anna

The lodger and I eventually worked out a housework rota, which basically has each of us doing three ten-minute to half-hour-long tasks each week. The house may not be the tidiest or cleanest place in the world, but what we do keeps it at an acceptable level and doesn't require us to be forever cleaning (which neither of us is in a position to do – she has chronic fatigue, and until recently I was working full-time with an hour and a half's commute each way).

Divide your housework into small tasks (Hoover the lounge, clean the kitchen surfaces, mop the kitchen floor), give both yourself and your partner one to do per day, and give yourself a small treat for doing it (even if it's only self-praise!).

ceiswyn

I bribed/encouraged my daughter to put her toys away by getting big pink boxes on wheels to keep everything in, and she's more than happy to dance around with me while I kick things under the settee, return things to shelves and have a quick tidy round!

madeleine

Go into a couple of rooms and identify one thing that could be done quickly and make the room look better, e.g. if there's a pair of trousers in the middle of the living room floor it'll only take a moment to remove them. Or set a timer and do five minutes per room.

mollydot

FELINE FOOT FETISHIST

Cat people, I need your help. I have a minor 'problem' with my youngest, Aubrey.

To put it mildly, Aubrey appears to be a feline foot fetishist. She keeps attacking our feet – or rather the Mr's feet – when we're in bed. Just pouncing on them would be bad enough, but she actually reaches under the duvet and gets you with claws on naked flesh. So the Mr is currently shutting her out of the bedroom at night, which is fine until about 5 am, when she starts

scratching the door. And it's Muggins here who wakes up!

So we're both sleep deprived and annoyed, which has led to us snapping at each other.

jules

All cats do this, in my experience. And it can be hard to train them out of it, because the kitty pouncing on the movement under the duvet is CUTE. However, if you can resist the cute it's not too hard to train the cat out of it. Just smack her/use the squirt bottle/fling her across the room/use your own preferred 'don't do that' method every single time she does it. She'll get the idea fairly fast, though she may need the occasional reminder. (Cats can learn 'I must not do that', but usually interpret it as 'I must not do that when the humans are around to see', and every so often will try doing it again in case the humans might have forgotten or not be looking!)

Good luck!

dorian

I've tried the letting the cats roam thing, the wanting them to sleep on the bed thing, and each time gone back to the norm in this household, which is that the cats sleep in baskets in the kitchen, which has their catflap to the outside, and the door between kitchen and rest of house stays shut overnight. Otherwise, I get miaowed at loudly till I wake up, trampled on till I wake up, purred and dribbled into my ear till I wake up, clawed on the face till I wake up. Shutting the bedroom door results in what you've found – scratching and miaowing at said door by kitty(s).

Shutting them into the kitchen means I can't hear the scratching/miaowing (which actually doesn't exist, since this is normality for them ever since kittenhood). I don't think it's unpleasant for them, either – they have free access in/out as they please, food, comfy baskets etc. etc. And, they don't get a crotchety human as often, either.

velvetpurrs

We never found a way to break Cobber of the foot thing. However, to break my cats of the scratching at the door thing I used a squirty water bottle. If you go and open the door they get the result they want, which is getting into your room. If you open the door as soon as you can when they start scratching, and spray them, they (often) quickly learn that actually they don't want the door to open and leave it alone.

k425

SEALANT

When using any kind of sealant/crack filler
whether plastic or plaster based, on woodwork,
tiles or whatever, taking the time to smooth it
really well (run a wet fingertip along the line of the
sealant) makes a huge difference, as any rough/
jagged edges will attract dirt and (in any vaguely
damp environment) mould like a magnet.

For a proper seal round baths/shower trays/
sinks, fire a load in as you fit them, let it go off,
and then do a final one all nice and smooth.
Always use silicone based as this allows flex.
For a sharp, clean edge use electrical tape as a
masking tape.

muggsy

SMELLY CAT

My cat stinks!!!

We acquired two 8-year-old
female cats a few months ago and one of them
constantly peed and pooed in the lounge. She's
been fine for ages and used her litter tray, but
since we've been away on holiday, she's using the

lounge again. **The whole downstairs of the house reeks! We moved all the furniture yesterday, washed and scrubbed the carpets, and she peed on it again. How do I stop her doing this? How do I get rid of the awful smell? The health visitor is coming next week for her first home visit and I don't want our house to smell of cat pee.**
   Help!

anna

It's possible that your cat is not merely peeing or pooing where convenient for her, but is actually marking her territory. If this is the case, every time you clean up she'll go back and do it again, unless you can find a way to discourage her. First, try and make sure you get rid of all traces of smell; a lot of vets sell product especially made for getting rid of animal urine or poo, so it might be a good idea to get one of these. Second, try a dab of orange oil in areas where she tends to pee or poo: cats are really not keen on the smell and will tend to keep away from it. Third, get yourself a water pistol, and if you see her peeing or pooing where she shouldn't, squirt her and shout 'NO' loudly. She won't like it, and she will learn quickly (and it's not cruel in the way that smacking her would be).
   If that doesn't work, I would suggest keeping her out of the lounge unless you're in there to supervise.

sushidog

Orange oil is very good – we resorted to using tiger balm when our lady cat was marking – but also, get her checked for cystitis. Some cats only do this when they're stressed or ill.

We steamed our carpets and the Vax'd them with Pet Rescue – it's a carpet shampoo thing that vets stock.

cookwitch

GETTING RID OF INSECTS

If you're phobic about insects or arachnids and there's no-one at hand to get rid of the object of your phobia, use the Hoover! Take the 'head' off, extend the hose as far as it will go, and you can suck up the little nasty from a safe distance. (This is not kind to the critter, but it beats sitting on the doorstep for five hours waiting for someone to come home and deal with it for you!)

dorian

TOMATO PLANTS

I have three tomato plants. This is the first year I've ever had them, so I'm on a high learning curve.

Will they survive over the winter, to bloom again next year? Or should I just rip them out now, and have done with it?

feath

They will probably die. They don't last outside in this country. No harm in trying though.

If you left some fruit on them to fall onto the ground, you may get new seedlings coming up of their own accord next year, but because of seed science they might not fruit as well as shop-bought specimens or seeds.

I had one self-seeder on my allotment that was very tasty but a lot less prolific than the ones I planted on purpose.

Did you know that tomato seeds are one of the few seeds that survive passage through the human gut? If you have a leak around your septic tank, it'll probably be full of tomato seedlings come the spring.

kg

DIY TIP

When hammering small nails into a wall or wood, to prevent 'blind cobbler's thumb' pain, hold the nail with your fingernails against the wall – that way, when you miss the nail you'll hit your fingertip pads not your fingernails, and it doesn't cause you to cry like a baby.

aychem o'twelfe

TEETHING KITTEN

Why does my adorable kitten (now 8 months) use me and only me as his chew toy? He loves to come and chew my fingers, and especially likes to try and drag one of them off! If it wasn't firmly attached I dread to think what he would do. He is a typical naughty kitten, always dragging things off and have a little chew – hair scrunchies, earbuds, even quite large things, and don't get me started on the subject of his apparent peacock feather fetish, but I am the only living thing he seems to want to chew. Any ideas?

pumpkin

Eight months is the shedding his milk teeth stage, so expect not only chewing but also finding very small kitten teeth around the house!

jz

If the kitten takes your finger in his mouth, push. Down his throat, block his airway. Works on most biting animals, actually. The kitten won't make you do it more than a few times – he'll have incentive to learn.

sol

CHRISTMAS DECORA-TIONS

Panel pins knocked into the wall in strategic places (e.g. picture rail if you have one) are great for stringing lights, chains or tinsel about the walls/around the windows and doors – and after the decorations come down, can either stay there almost unnoticeably, or be pulled out very easily and without making a huge mess.

dorian

COOKING GOOSE

How do I cook my Christmas goose?

vf

Make sure it's completely dry before you cook it. Take it out of the fridge to come to room temperature and pat it dry with kitchen roll before putting it in the oven. Don't add butter or lard.

If you have stuffed it, weigh it with the stuffing to calculate the cooking time. Don't use a fatty stuffing inside the bird, like sausage meat – something made of apples or parsnips is good. Bread-based stuffings dry turkey out but work well in goose.

For timings, Delia Smith suggests 'Give it 30 minutes' initial cooking, then reduce the temperature to gas mark 4, 350°F (180°C) and give it another three hours. That's for an 11 lb (5 kg) goose plus stuffing: allow 15 minutes less for 10 lb (4.5 kg); 15 minutes more for 12 lb (5.4 kg).' Most importantly, cook it on a rack so that the fat can drain into the pan underneath. Otherwise it will be fatty and icky.

I am envious – I much prefer goose to turkey!

pp

If you have stuffed it, weigh it with the stuffing to calculate the cooking time.

Is this true of all big roasts? We do cook chicken/ duck/game birds at home on occasion, but those are far smaller birds, for just the two of us + several meals afterwards, where 'cook until done' is a bit less of a timing risk.

We're 'doing' Christmas, and I have The Fear over the turkey (boy thinks I'm being irrational, and is merrily reporting back: 'Oh yeah, Mum thinks we'll need an approx 14 lb bird, does that sound about right?'; I'm wondering whether taking a tape measure to the supermarket to check it'll fit in the oven is a bit mad or just common sense.

We did discover a rather comedy thing though with duck – stuffed with one of the nice Sainsbury's Taste the Difference stuffings, failed to spot the 'leave for 15 minutes' instructions and shoved it straight in the oven after mixing with water – turned out lovely, but the expanding stuffing broke the bird right along the breastbone, so we ended up with very clever-looking roast with crispy stuffing right down the middle, as if it had burst its buttons! I've no idea whether it was a weird once-off or whether duck skeletons are always brittle enough to do that.

sea_of_flame

Is this true of all big roasts?

Absolutely. Stuffings add to the cooking time. Some people say you shouldn't put stuffing in the body cavity because it slows down the cooking so much and there is a danger the meat will be under-cooked. But as long as you remember to add enough time it should be fine.

The other problem with stuffing a large bird is that it takes a long time for the heat to penetrate and cook the stuffing and interior of the bird, whereas the breast cooks relatively quickly. So by the time your bird is cooked through, the breast is overdone and dry. One solution to this is to roast it breast-down for most of the time and turn it over towards the end. This helps to keep the breast moist. Another solution, which I will try this year, is to soak the bird in a spiced brine for a day or two before drying and cooking it.

14lb bird, does that sound about right?

I'm doing dinner for six and I've got a 6.8 kg (15 lb) turkey on order, which I'm hoping will give us plenty of leftovers. I have been assured that this will fit in a standard domestic oven with room to spare for the spuds and neeps. Taking a tape measure sounds very sensible to me!

pp

Keep it moist both inside and out – apple stuffing + lots of pancetta wrapping courtesy of Gordon Ramsey and Nigel Slater is the way forward. Using a dripping rack is essential.

genie22

GARDENING

I have been toying with the idea of a veg plot and herb garden for a while, and as we won't be moving for the foreseeable future now seems as good a time as any. What I would like to ask is whether anyone here has a veg plot/herb garden

but would consider themselves NOT green fin-gered, and not normally motivated to tend such things, and how you get around these problems and achieve good results. I work full time, and while I love home-grown veg, I have no time to fuss over them.

pumpkin

Pick things that don't require much effort – fruit trees if you have space and you're lingering. Rhubarb, once settled, gives fuss-free early fruit. Courgettes in grow-bags need watering regularly but not much else, and give you a heck of a lot of veg for minimal effort. Mooli (giant white radish) is really easy to grow and gives a massive quantity for minimal effort – quick too, and doesn't seem to bolt like ordinary radish. Beetroot can be pretty easy too.

For herbs avoid annuals and dump perennials in the ground. Thyme, rosemary, sage, oregano, mint and chives need only be planted once and then can be left to get on with it.

caffeine_fairy

Fruit is easier than veg, and needs less attention.

Herbs can safely be ignored for weeks on end, but grow them in pots unless you want nothing but herbs in your garden.

Potatoes are easy and you can grow them in a stack of tires if you don't like digging. Runner beans are dead easy and quite pretty to look at.

Good luck! Alan Titchmarsh's *How to be a Gardener* is excellent and gives really low-maintenance options for growing veg.

md

I planted mini sweetcorn last year – the plant grows to the same size as normal corn, and, to be quite honest, my mini cobs weren't really much smaller than normal ones! I suspect I Did Something Wrong but that it worked for the right reasons – my idea of care for them was to plant them round the edges of the trough and throw water at them on a semi-regular basis.

This year I am trying cauliflower, broccoli and peppers (oh, and tomatoes, of course, they're very easy) in growbags in the garden. I'm quite excited by it! I have a miniature cherry tree too, and am looking forward to that flowering and fruiting!

bunnyk

I LOVE WASHING SODA!

I have been a fan of washing soda for some time. It's the best thing I know for dealing with burned pots and manky grill-pans. Today, I found/invented a new use for it, which I want to share with all of you.

Got burned/stuck-on dirt on your cooker-top, draining board (insert other place that can't be conveniently soaked)? Here's how to deal with it.

Dump about half a cupful of washing soda into a saucer and add a teeny-tiny bit of hot water to make a paste. Apply this paste to the stubborn dirt. Go away and have a cup of tea/read a bit/watch some telly/whatever for half an hour. After *at least* half an hour, return and scrub the offending area with a pot-scourer (not rinsing or anything first). The dirt should come off fairly easily. Rinse/wipe/etc. Hey presto, sparkly-clean whatever-it-was!

(I cleaned my draining board for the first time in about a year today, used this method for the bits that wouldn't come clean with kitchen-spray-with-bleach and elbow-grease, and yay! Clean draining board!)

dorian

Sex and Sexual Health

CONDOM ADVICE

http://www.bigboycondoms.co.uk/ has a wide
range of condoms for sale online

cookwitch

WHAT YOU SHOULD KEEP AND WHAT THROW AWAY IN A NEW RELATIONSHIP

Hmm, I would say underwear is a keeper, unless it's
specifically for the bedroom rather than for actually

wearing, in which case I'm not sure; I've never had bedroom-only undies!

Toys for solo use are keepers, but I can see how toys for dual use might not be, particularly if they are 'intimate' in use for the other partner; so, for example, a vibrator which your partner has used on you is probably OK to keep, but one which was used (for insertion) on him (or her) might not be.

sushidog

On the toys front, I suspect that if I ever found out that a boyfriend had brought something to bed that had been used with the previous girlfriend in any form, I think I'd probably throw a small fit (or indeed quite a large one) because it would feel rather like inviting her ghost into bed.

elle

As far as toys go, I think it depends on the nature of the toy and the length of the relationship it was bought during. On the whole though, I do think if it was bought for the 'you' as a couple then I do think its kinda odd to use it again with someone else. But using a clit vibrator or handcuffs with a different person is much easier to live with than using something that penetrates.

smallblakflower

SEX TOY ADVICE

http://www.sh-womenstore.com/ for sex toys

quorta

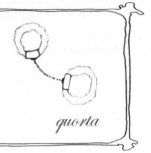

BUYING AND USING BONDAGE TAPE

Ann Summers definitely sell some. What one does with it, though, I have no idea.

bee

Sh! stocks it, and if you talk to them they will give you lots of advice.

quorta

Pallet wrap is that really wide, long stuff (known as bitch wrap thanks to a friend of mine!). The stuff is really good, it can be big enough to cocoon a whole body, and is very difficult to wriggle out of!

My ex had bondage tape (why is it always the ex?) and managed to cut off the blood supply to my wrists when he dropped the end down the back of the bed! Didn't notice at the time, but sure did later – pins and needles are not a fun sex aid!

I've seen it used for dresses and some beautiful bondage displays – just have fun with it! Though I think you have to wind it really, really tight, and I don't think I've ever seen it on anyone over a size 6 either (grrr). But then it did have 'go faster' stripes down each side, so they may have helped to keep it together. I prefer rope anyway, it's more um... interesting!

jules

No good for wearing out as boob cover if you have small boobs like mine though. Squishes them in too much.

batswing

KEEPING THE FLAME ALIVE

Spend time together before having sex – go for a light meal, go and have a walk and a chat, a couple of drinks at the pub – whatever as long as you have each other's undivided attention in a fairly calm atmosphere and you're chatting. Don't eat or drink too much.

Don't tell yourself that you're worried about discomfort – try to visualise yourself having fun. Be vocal if it's hurting – there's nothing wrong with saying 'that hurts a bit, can we stop for a while and do something else?' You'll resent it if you grit your teeth and bear it.

Don't try and 'get it over with' – penetrative sex will hurt more and not be pleasurable without sufficient foreplay. Have lube near to hand too.

If it doesn't happen, don't beat yourselves up about it, you can always try again. Talk about it: there's nothing wrong with saying 'Ooh yes that's lovely, keep doing it' or 'Just a minute, that doesn't feel quite right'.

Remember that the pill and other medications, such as antidepressants, can lower your libido.

na

WHAT IS SEX?

What do you define as 'sex'?

As a bisexual woman, for example, I'd count oral sex as sex, but I've known straight women who automatically assumed that sex equalled penis-in-vagina.

ha

For me, when I'm defining it as something I do myself, it's PIV, PIA (both ways, i.e. both me-on-him and him-on-me), FIA etc. I tend to count non-penetrative sexual stuff as more a kind of 'extended fooling around'. I'm not a huge fan of oral so I rarely get round to thinking about it!

As for other people, when they talk about 'sex' I usually assume they define it themselves so I don't like to presume.

lozette

Contact with genitalia, resulting in pleasure!

We had this conversation a while ago when a friend was describing a one-night stand to me and my girl-friend. She claimed that they were naked and stuff happened, but 'they didn't have sex'. I looked at my girlfriend. 'They had sex,' she clarified.

'NO! We didn't! We didn't have sex!' she exclaimed in horror.

'Don't worry dear, we were just translating into lesbian,' we explained.

la bias

Anything that I wouldn't talk to my mother about in detail.

tooth_fairy

Sex results in a particular form of arousal and satisfaction. Like gender, it appears to be simple on the surface but is in fact more a state of mind than a physical, immutable, reality.

blue_cat

Sex = anything that gets you aroused and results in enjoyment of one form or another. Nice simple definition that covers most situations from self-love to orgies.

caturah

With men, the only thing I'd consider sex is penis-in-vagina.

I find it kind of confusing really! Like, if I had oral sex with a woman and oral sex with a man, I wouldn't say I'd had sex with a man, so I wouldn't say I'd had sex with the woman.

glassarmy

Sex is two or more people proceeding with intent towards one or more orgasms.

sushidog

I think my definition would be quite broad, although I can't quite work out where my boundaries are. Certainly I'd include getting naked together, but even that isn't really necessary: anything intended for the pleasure of the other partner, maybe?

Maybe that's rather too broad, though. I think I'm having a hard job disentangling sex and physical intimacy and anything I'd consider infidelity if it were with anyone other than my partner. I'm fairly sure that there are things that come under 'infidelity' but not 'sex', but I can't entirely work out what distinguishes them.

nounou

'I did not have sex with that woman' may have been valid by Clinton's standards, but I tend to define 'sex' as one or all of:

- Manual–genital contact resulting in orgasm (or attempting to do so)
- Oral–genital contact ditto
- Genital–genital contact (any)
- Any activity designed to result in orgasm (or attempting to do so), e.g. frottage.

I'm not always quite clear about defining cybersex etc. as 'sex' even though it may result in orgasm.

vampwillow

I'm almost-entirely-straight-by-practice, and I define sex as any kind of extended★ activity aiming to give sexual pleasure, with someone else (I don't really count solo masturbation as sex, but mutual, sure). I like PIV, but it's not the most fun bit so it seems bizarre to consider that the be-all and end-all. *i.e. not just a quick grope.

gj

Hmm. I have trouble with this because I had oral sex with my first boyfriend, but always feel I 'lost my virginity' to my third.

This definition is pretty hard-wired in my head, and I'm not going to start saying I lost it to the first guy. I just... didn't. There was no penetrative sex, none of the 'will it hurt?' sentiments or bleeding afterwards that happen when you actually do lose your virginity. But in subsequent relationships I'd define any sort of sex as sex. And yes, it normally takes me months of getting to know a guy I'm shagging before I'll give him a blowjob.

starmix

I'm bi too. For me, in an m/f relationship 'sex' means 'His penis is in my vagina, and he has an orgasm.' For an f/f relationship it means 'anything that produces sexual pleasure (hopefully culminating in one or more orgasms) for both of us'.

lothie

Can't remember who said it, but I've always liked 'Sex is any activity you walk away from thinking 'I got laid'.'

slemslempike

GETTING A CLITORAL PIERCING

Apparently in some cases clitoral piercing can reduce sensation fairly drastically, whereas clitoral hood piercings tend to increase it and are generally safer.

sushidog

I highly rate Cold Steel in Camden, where I had my tongue pierced. Go somewhere like Cold Steel or Metal Morphosis, somewhere where they are known as top-quality piercers and have a lot of experience of this. Sadly, my favourite piercing (nipple) was done at Rings of Desire in New Orleans, but hell, if you're ever passing there...

kauket

I had my vertical hood piercing done at Cold Steel, and they were really excellent. The piercer was very friendly and calming, and really good about explaining what was going to happen and how to keep things clean. I wasn't offered a freezing spray, but honestly it wasn't very painful at all. The actual piercing bit was over very quickly, and then the rest of the day I barely felt a thing.

I'm in Manchester now, and I had my nipples pierced at 'Holier than Thou', and I would really recommend them too – really great staff, very patient when I suddenly had a slight wibble beforehand!

stemstempike

I got mine done at Cold Steel in Camden. Also clitoral hood. I found that it hurt A LOT; but I had (still have to some extent) Issues about medical-type procedures in that area. The point of the piercing was partly a kind of reaction against that, and it did sort-of work. So, yeah, everyone else I know has said that it hardly hurt at all, and it certainly didn't hurt for *long* – only a fraction of a second. It healed up very fast (salt baths helped!). And I would certainly recommend Cold Steel.

I wound up taking mine out a couple of years later, as I found that it made me somewhat oversensitive and didn't have the side-benefits I'd been hoping for!

jk

I got my clitoral hood pierced four months ago and it's fab. I would definitely recommend that rather than a clitoral piercing. All the benefits without the risks. I got mine done at the Manchester and Leeds Piercing Studio (near Afflecks Palace, Manchester) www.bo-dypiercing.co.uk. I have had piercings done at Cold Steel in London as well and they are excellent.

tooth_fairy

SEX BOOK RECOM-MENDATION

I have found that *The Good Vibrations Guide to Sex* covers the basics on pretty much everything and I heartily recommend it. It also has extensive links for further information and a good bibliography.

tooth_fairy

BDSM

May I present you with http://www.informed consent.co.uk – should you be up for a browse?

ni

MISSED PILL

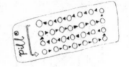

Advice needed, asap! Started my pill a day late this month, should have started Tuesday. Had sex last night, five days after missed pill. I know you're supposed to use some other form of contraception for seven days after a missed pill, but I'm not sure if it's as important with the first one.

I've taken the morning-after pill before and it made me ill, had awful cramps for a fortnight, so not keen! But obviously, not a clever risk to take. So, basically, I'm not sure if I should go get the morning-after pill.

mc

You can get it from behind the counter of a chemist's. It's only one day of being ill, compared to a lifetime of being a mother. Or ask to see a nurse practitioner if you can't get in with a doctor – they'll be able to jump the queue for you. Also, I believe you could get it from A&E, but they give you funny looks.

vf

As I understand it, missing a pill at the beginning or the end of your pack is higher risk than missing one in the middle. You're *probably* OK, but if I were you I'd go get the morning-after pill sharpish.

sk

I think the morning-after pill becomes less effective if you take it after 24 hours, so best to try to get it as soon as possible. You should be able to get an appointment with the doctor or nurse fairly quickly, although some doctors aren't so good at that kind of thing. An advantage of going to the doctor for it is that they can give you anti-nausea tablets and such, which might make you feel less ill. I wonder if the GUM clinic gives prescriptions for it? Maybe. If you can't get an appointment with the doctor/nurse, it might be worth trying them.

judith_crunch

If you're a student you can get it over the counter free from your local sexual health clinic, and from your student institution. If not, try the local practice nurse or A&E for free ones. SHC will be the only confidential one. Do it fast – the effectiveness of the pill drops considerably after 24 hours. Though most advertise till 72 hours, at that point effectiveness is only 9%. Unless you feel you're in the right place to have a child, take the pill not the risk.

ebee

GETTING THE MORNING-AFTER PILL FROM A CHEMIST

Any big pharmacy will sell it to you. They will ask you questions though, BUT they do that in private.

cookwitch

They'll get you to make an appointment in Boots, but it's free. They do ask you questions about where you are in your cycle, if you've taken it before, if so did you have a bad reaction, and such forth. They'll also ask general medical questions, like are you prone to headaches, blackouts, fainting etc. But presuming they don't see any problem with any of your answers then you'll get the pill. The problem is the waiting time for the appointment. I went to a Boots once for one and was told I'd have to wait five days – um, hello, it only works within 78 hours/three days?!

Superdrug will also give you the pill BUT they'll charge you about £20. However, no appointment. Though you do have to go through another medical questionnaire.

I think it's also free from the NHS walk-in centres, but you've gotta sit around all day waiting to be seen and of course they're doctors, so they might go the whole hog with examinations and lectures and such.

sara

Yup... it's free from walk-in centres, doctors, family planning clinics, university sick bays and med centres, and I have a vague memory that you might be able to get them from A&E (as most of the others aren't open after hours).

silvernik

Boots have the NHS Walk-In Centre, where if you make an appointment you'll be able to get it free. If you get it over the counter at the pharmacy, you'll have to pay. The only brand in the UK at the moment is Levonelle, which is £25. Even if you get it over the counter you'll have to have a quiet chat with the pharmacist, but that can be done in private and they're very nice!

*_mardybum_*

Does anyone know whether you can buy it in advance in order to have it around for when you might need it? Because that would seem vaguely sensible.

sk

Yes you can buy it in advance... part of the promotion of it was so that women could buy it and have it in their medicine cabinet. Of course the arguments against this were that women would use it instead of contraception.

silvernik

GETTING A BAD REACTION TO THE MORNING-AFTER PILL

I would strongly advise anyone who had a bad reaction to go to their local well-woman clinic, or make an appointment with their practice nurse, and ask about their options for contraception; they'll be able to give an expert opinion and explain all the possibilities, as well as giving advice on reactions to the MAP!

sushidog

I have only taken it once and it affected me both psychologically and physically for a while, but I did call NHS Direct for advice before and after taking it – give them a try (that's if you are in the UK): 0845

4647; if you are not in the UK, have a look at the website http://www.nhsdirect.nhs.uk/.

pumpkin

The MAP is essentially a whopping dose of hormones, so unfortunately, feeling like crap is to be expected. Lots of tea, hot water bottles and painkillers are a good idea.

pipistrellus

IMPLANON EFFECTS

I just got poked with a large Implanon (contraceptive) stick about an hour ago. Side effects could include bleeding from every orifice for a year and a half, or they could include no periods at all, no body odour of any sort, a thick and glossy coat, a sudden talent for arranging flowers, and the ability to do magic. We'll see which end of the scale I end up on. I know where my bets are.

offensive_mango

I had a Depo shot a few years ago... guess which end of the side effects spectrum I came under.

I went back to the doctor after I'd been bleeding for several months and he said 'I could give you another shot when it's due and that *might* solve things, or it could get worse'. I decided to tell him where to shove it.

elizabeth

I had one and was quite happy with it, but the removal wasn't pleasant. Silly woman doing the removal messed it up and it took ages. Grr.

emily

I tried Depo a few years ago and my friend also opted to give it a go around the same time. Neither of us ever managed to shed the huge amount of weight we gained.

pipistrellus

I like the shot, I only have to worry about it every three months. But I put weight on. Wonder if coming off it would get rid of the weight?

kauket

Absolutely great in terms of periods (oh, the hardship of suffering the side effect of 'not getting them') – however, I've had it for getting on for three years and my sex drive has dropped very noticeably during about the last year/18 months.

The good thing about Implanon is that because it's a physical slow-release thing, if you don't get on with it they can take it out and things settle back to normal fairly rapidly (in theory immediately, but I would guess that practically there's a short period of hormones settling down, as there would be if you came off the pill or similar, just because of residual amounts still in your system), whereas the shot is instantly in the system for three months, like it or not.

Keep the pressure bandage on, no matter how much the bloody thing itches – it really will keep the bruising to a minimum.

sea_of_flame

COIL

I have a coil, the copper one without hormones, and have had it for almost five years. It was not comfortable to insert – there was a great feeling of pressure in the abdomen, sort of like a series of intense period cramps, but I did lots of deep breathing which helped, and since then apart from mid-cycle spotting for the first month I haven't had any problems with it.

Before insertion they run through a whole series of tests to check that you don't have any diseases or infections that can be compounded by the coil. I don't really know all the pros and cons, but I've been super-happy with mine. I don't feel it, and neither does my partner.

rainsinger

I have had the Mirena coil for two or three years now (the one with hormones) and have been really happy with it. I went off the pill because it killed my sex drive and have had no such problem with the coil (the amount of hormones is tiny). I can't feel it and neither could my ex (I'm single now, so it's not getting much use anyway). I barely have periods now (although I do still have the side effects of them – just don't really bleed) and am very happy with it.

It does hurt to have it put in and I had strong period-like cramps for a couple of days afterwards. Since then no trouble though, so stock up on nice painkillers and hot water bottles etc. for those couple of days.

The doctor had no problem fitting me with one (Mirena coils are a lot less problematic in general than the older-style ones) and you don't have to have had children first in order to get one.

hyzenflay

I've got a Mirena and I love it. I'm in the lucky 25% of users that get no periods whatsoever with it, which is a nice bonus.

If you've never given birth vaginally then you might have a slightly harder time convincing them to fit one for you, and you may have to go to a special 'coil clinic' (usually at the hospital) to get it fitted, rather than the doc just popping it in.

I actually went to a sexual health clinic for mine, rather than the GP, on the grounds that someone who fits IUDs as a significant portion of their job is going to be more experienced at it than a random GP.

Insertion was uncomfortable but no worse than that for me. You can take some paracetamol and/or ibuprofen in advance if you're worried.

vicky l

I've had the Mirena coil since March last year and love it. Like Vicky L, I don't seem to bleed while on it (or at least I had one very light bleed after the fitting and not since). One of the GPs at my practice specialises in fitting them, and has a specific time each week for doing so, when a nurse assists her. I find it suits me very well: I can't forget it, I can't lose it, I tend to forget about it entirely for weeks at a time, and it means I can't get pregnant without making a positive decision to do so.

One thing I should mention is the issue of the strings. There are two little thin plastic strings that hang down from the IUS and out of your cervix, which you can feel every month or two to make sure that the coil is still inside, and which the doctors use to remove it. My boyfriend found he could feel them too and they were hurting him, but when I went for my follow-up appointment a month later, the doctor was happy to trim them a little.

My strings have gone AWOL recently – probably retreated inside the cervix – and I'm currently waiting for an ultrasound scan to check the Mirena is still there and correctly positioned.

rmc28

Thanks for being so frank – I've heard some horror stories from people who've had either an IUD or an IUS fitted about how much it hurt etc., and stories like this are quite scary if it's something you're considering (which I most definitely am – my doctor said that she herself had one fitted, as did 90% of the female doctors she knew even if they hadn't had children).

I know people's pain thresholds are different, which

might account for the different stories I've heard –
uncomfortable I can put up with, though!

sera_squeak

STERILISA-TION

**I'm seriously considering sterilisation. I don't
want kids, and I have never found contraception
that really suits me (my current pill is the best so
far, but is still not ideal). For those of you who
have had this done, what sort of hoops did you
have to jump through to get doctors to agree to
it, and what were the waiting lists like? Also, does
anyone have any useful links? Thanks.**

sd

I knew somebody who managed to get herself steril-
ised in her mid-20s some time ago (she was older than
me). She had to work hard to convince the medical
profession that she really, really didn't want kids.

juggzy

Marie Stopes will do it for £700, if you can afford
that, and have minimal hoops. I think they do require
that you see a counsellor pre-op, but only one appointment (to make sure, presumably, that you really
are aware of what you're doing, which is fair enough).

jk

I had mine done on the NHS when I was 24 (23 through all the consults). I had to jump through a few hoops, but I was prepared to as I *was* pretty young. A lot also depends on which gynaecologist you get referred to and what their attitude is!

If you go via the NHS you don't usually get a choice of who you get referred to. As for waiting times, again that just depends on how busy the gynae you see is. I had to wait three months, which was fine.

lozette

I asked my doctor about it when I was 24 and just married – I've known I didn't want kids since I was 5 or 6. It took four years, two doctors, two gynaecologists and a psychologist before the NHS finally agreed I did know my own mind, and I had it done last summer at the Mayday Hospital in Croydon.

cazmanian minx

DEPO-RELATED WEIGHT LOSS

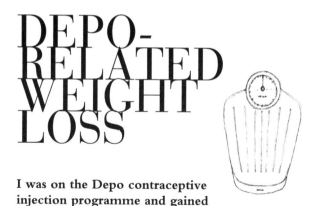

I was on the Depo contraceptive injection programme and gained over half a stone in weight. Following two or

three injections I decided to stop. This was two months ago or so. I still haven't got my periods yet, but that's OK because it can take up to a year to 'get back to normal'. However, I am trying very hard to lose the weight I had put on and it seems to be going very slowly, despite my eating in a very healthy way and exercising from 40 to 80 minutes (cardiovascular) five times a week. I am wondering whether the hormones that may still be in my body might be mucking things up for me, or whether I am being impatient. But in a month of doing this I would have expected to lose more than just 2 lb.

siren

It depends on how big you are to start with, and how radical the change in lifestyle. If you're not particularly overweight and eat healthily generally, then 2 lb is quite a lot.

How do you look and feel? With that regular exercise you're building muscle that is heavier than fat, but your body will look the better for it.

md

I'm not doing weight training, which I used to do in my old gym: I generally either run or cross-train as hard as I can go. I'm not fat, but since putting on the weight I feel unhappy about the way I look, mainly because I suddenly have this sticky-out stomach. I always did eat healthily really, but the exercise is dramatically more than I used to do. I walk 20 minutes to work and 20 minute home again five times a week, but now I have been adding 45 minutes of hardcore cardiovascular to that three or four times a week.

siren

Probably the increase in exercise, regardless of it not being weight training, will have added muscle. You have probably lost more fat than you think, and you will probably lose more weight in the coming month, as your body will have got used to the extra exercise.

tooth_fairy

It may be time to ditch the scales – if you're not fat they'll only mislead and demoralize you.

If you're tummy is bugging you, maybe look into exercise that specifically targets and tones the tum (Pilates is great for that). The CV work you're doing is going to give you great legs, and the tum will follow (honest!) just rather more slowly.

md

When I started exercising I didn't see any improvement for the first month, but then I started to notice a visible improvement. I would say to be patient and stick with it. 40–80 minutes' CV five times a week is excellent – good going.

lannie

Instead of just using the scales to monitor progress, also use a tape measure and measure the loss that way too. If you are doing a lot of exercise and building up muscle tone, you might find that you are losing fat and inches, it just doesn't show up on the scales, because as several people have pointed out, muscle weighs more than fat.

ad

A few comments:

Even if you're only doing CV and not weight-training you'll probably be building up muscle to a certain extent. Muscle is denser than fat, and if you're replacing fat with muscle you wouldn't see much change in actual weight – if you measure yourself you may find you've actually got smaller.

'Healthy' food doesn't necessarily equal low-calorie: for years I couldn't understand why I didn't lose weight despite exercising and eating extremely healthily, until I started calorie-counting and weigh-ing all my food and realised just how many calories the size of bowl of pasta I'd been eating contained! On the other hand, if you're restricting food intake significantly and doing all that exercise, it's possible that you're actually consuming too *few* calories for successful weight loss – if you eat too little your body will go into 'starvation mode' and assume that there's a famine, so it will try to hold on to fat stores even more. You need to make sure that you have a net calorie intake (after deducting calories burnt through exercise from calories consumed) of over 1100 per day. Around 1500 is recommended for steady, safe weight loss.

wh

First of all, well done for sticking to your exercise routine and healthy eating! I agree with the comments above that you're probably putting on muscle at the moment. This will make you weigh more but it will make the exercise easier – making strong muscles stronger is much easier than making weak muscles strong.

If shifting a spare tyre is a problem then you might have to do specific exercises that help that area. This doesn't necessarily mean sit-ups, but they're the quickest way of achieving it! It might be worth investing in a sit-up frame if sit-ups tend to make your back hurt, as they help correct your 'posture'. Other good tummy-toning stuff: lie on your back and lift your ankles off the ground about 1–2 ft and hold there. Repeat until bored. Some yoga exercises are also good – I love yoga but don't get to practise it much these days – I would heartily recommend it for enjoyable, relaxing exercise, and if you get a video you can do it in your front room! Pilates is a little more intensive but very good for targeting specific areas. Then there's the tried and tested 'sitting-at-desk clench' which you can do all day if you so wish.

ks

Stomachs and healthy eating: if you're eating a lot of healthy fibre-laden stuff, it's quite likely there's a fair bit of volume working its way through your digestive system – there's just quite a lot in there taking up room, you know? If you're fairly slim already it'll show. Not much to do about that, but be pleased about having a well-functioning body.

By way of example, I look noticeably slimmer when I've had a terrible hangover and haven't eaten for most of the day. Slim isn't the same as healthy.

shermarama

I reckon getting your periods back will be the best indication of when your body has recovered. It took me between three and six months to get back to normal after less than a year on the combined pill, so I wouldn't be surprised if it still took a while for you to 'recover'.

sera_squeak

INDUCING PERIODS

Where is it? My period still hasn't come – I've worked it out loads of times now and it's definitely 33 days since my last one – though I did have a little bleeding in between, about two days after the period stopped but it was because of something else. I have done a pregnancy test and it was negative. But where is my period? Any hints on making it start?

I am not on any sort of pill – but I did take Levonelle a few months ago.

elethe

When did you do the pregnancy test? It might be worth doing another one, but chances are you're just having a late period. Try having a warm bath with a few drops of clary sage oil in it (it'll also help you sleep, though I find it gives me very odd dreams!), as this can often help to kick-start a late period.

sushidog

I did the test yesterday. I have tried hot baths, black cohosh, lots of coffee, agnus castus – not helped so far.

elethe

Raspberry leaf tea – I really think it helps.

tb

No secrets for bringing one on. How stressed were you two to three weeks ago? More than usual? Could just be a delayed ovulation due to stress, which would make you late but not pregnant.

mjf

MOONCUPS

A while ago, inspired by a thread in a feminist community, I bought a mooncup (http://www.mooncup.co.uk/). I've only used it once so far, but it's GREAT! Minimal fuss, eco-friendly, comfortable, and no risk of toxic shock. I was really worried I'd have trouble with it, but so far so good. It feels nice to be dealing with my periods in a kind of hip, lo-fi way, too.

tb

LATE PMS?

OK, my period arrived two days ago. Normally this is greeted with joy, since it means the end of horrible PMT, and I can always tell it's due because my mood improves substantially the day beforehand. But for the last two months I've needed the chocolate and tissues for several days in. Am sniffling now and hoovering up chocolate Minstrels. Does anyone else get this? It is normal to get PMS during your period too isn't it?

gg

I always need chocolate in the first 24 hours and feel extremely weepy and vulnerable.

mendi

Yes, it's entirely normal. I get PMS sometimes before my period, sometimes on the first day, and sometimes later in the period.

Premenstrual tension is one of those psychological syndromes that exists largely because people think it does. I think it was in the 1930s/1940s when it was named. Before then the thing was menstrual tension and the same symptoms tended to be reported during the period, in particular on the first day, not before it. Studies mapping moods throughout the month have shown that, for most women, there is no definite premenstrual tension. We may feel weepy or in need of chocolate at any time during the month – it's just that when it happens before a period we ascribe it to premenstrual tension rather than just feeling shitty or having had a crappy day, or whatever other external cause we may give it at other times of the month.

Obviously your hormones do change throughout the month and these can affect your mood, but this goes on throughout the month and not just right before your period. This is especially true if you aren't on the pill and therefore aren't affecting your hormones that way.

All of which is just me waving my intellectual knickers in the air (to use Stephen Fry's wonderful phrase) and is a very long-winded way of saying it's entirely normal to get mood swings and need chocolate throughout the month. Enjoy your Minstrels!

caroline

Yes, I get it really badly sometimes and want to howl and hide till a few days after. Someone speaking to me at the wrong time can send me off into rage, too. It's really nasty, and only chocolate and well-timed hugs can help. Oh, and Buffy singalongs, too.

batswing

PERIOD PAIN

Just wondering if anyone knew of any ways in which you can help lessen period pain – preferably natural ones. I've tried the hot water bottle and painkillers, and although the hot water bottle is nice, it's not practical for achieving anything other than watching stupid amounts of Buffy the Vampire Slayer.

notcollins

May sound a bit mad, but using cloth pads or a mooncup (www.mooncup.co.uk) seems to help a LOT of people to have less painful periods, don't know if it's physiological or psychological ('accepting your body' type thing) or what, but there is a lot of anecdotal evidence that supports it, plus it's cheaper and you don't get horrible dry sore skin from wearing lumps of plastic over your bits all week...

anwen

A warm damp flannel, with a few drops of fennel oil, placed over your abdomen. However, as with all essential oils, make sure you're not allergic or sensitive to it.

caturah

I strongly recommend evening primrose oil – I take it all the time, doubling the dose around ovulation.

Also, the little self-heating gel pads they sell in hiking shops are good; I can tuck one down the waist of my trousers and wander around the house OK. Oh, and swearing a lot.

ailbhe

Port. Seriously, for some reason, I find a glass of port really helps. Apparently Marmite is supposed to be helpful too, due to the vitamin B it contains.

Orgasms, if you can bear to get there. Warm baths, particularly with a few drops of lavender, marjoram or clary sage oil. Marjoram tends to zonk me out, so it's good if you're having trouble sleeping, but bad if you want to feel alert within the next 24 hours. Clary sage used when hormonal gives me extremely rude dreams, which may be a good thing or not, depending on you.

sushidog

I read in the *New Scientist* that they did a test on women using vitamin E – those who took it for the three days prior to and three days into their period had less pain. If you take evening primrose oil (a lifesaver for PMT), the capsule is made of vitamin E so it would kill two birds with one stone, so to speak.

Also, diet is very important in helping with PMT: you may crave chocolate and bad stuff like bread and cakes, but it's the worst thing you can eat at that time, as it will add to the general bloatedness and feeling crap. Oily fish, vegetables, all that sort of thing, should help. Wholegrains, if you can eat them, drink lots of liquids that aren't tea/coffee, and buy some Feminax.

It's got codeine, paracetamol and some anti-cramping agent (apparently) in it. If you can take codeine, that is. And a hot water bottle.

kg

I had several months on a triphasic pill/painkiller regime which sorted me out for ages afterwards. Now a strict regime of evening primrose oil every day and ibuprofen when necessary has improved things.

jz

My period pains – and they were really bad for a time – have become much less so since I've started doing regular exercise, make a point of including soy products of some sort in my diet (was using soy milk until I realised that you can get soy yoghurts and dry-roasted soy nuts in Sainsbury's) and generally try to avoid high GI foods. They haven't gone away completely, and if I eat badly or forget to exercise, they come back. I do think low GI diets help a lot.

juggzy

A herbal thing – have you tried vitex agnus castus and cramp bark, as tinctures? Heating pads are also a good thing. Or how about acupressure?

meepettemu

SUPPLEMENTS

My hormones are a bit skewed at the moment and I'm trying to get them to calm down a bit as I'm suffering horrendous PMT and other related miseries. In the past, evening primrose oil has done nothing for me, possibly made it worse, so I've tended to avoid it. I am now taking it again in the form of Well Woman capsules and have had no ill-effects, so am hoping that may help. However, I'm interested in any other supplements or foods or vitamins you've taken that have helped with PMT and general wellbeing. Any thoughts?

starmix

My mother tells me that starflower oil has a higher concentration of the active stuff (GLAs) that's in in evening primrose oil than evening primrose does. I don't take these things because I'm lazy and I forget, but my mother says they do her some good. Also B vitamin complexes are good for bad-temperedness (but take care if you're also taking another supplement – I don't know what the overdose is, but I wouldn't be very up for risking it!). My mother used to feed them to my very bad-tempered father without him knowing, and he'd usually be noticeably calmer. Only side effect I've had from B vitamins is that they turn your urine an alarming shade of green.

bee

Anything with B6 in it used to screw up my cycle. Starflower oil is very good, allegedly, but I find it best to cook something complicated and forget all about it.

duckiemonster

From personal experience cutting down on high-carb foods can help. Basic explanation: insulin is a hormone – high-carb foods can bugger up insulin – hence high-carb foods can bugger up hormones...

pumpkin

Vitex AGNUS CASTUS – wonderful stuff.

meepettemu

PERIODS AND EVENING PRIMROSE OIL

My period this month has been ridiculously light by my standards – like, two sanitary towels a day rather than the usual one-every-two-or-three-hours. No, this isn't a complaint!

I've been on the same Pill for over 10 years, and the only thing I can think of that's changed recently is that I've been taking **evening primrose oil** (because my breasts were aching all the time and a couple of people suggested it might help, though it doesn't seem to have done). It says something vague on the packet like 'Helps to keep your hormones in balance' – does that include making periods lighter? If so, then it may actually be worth the small fortune they charge for the stuff... (BTW I have looked on the web but most of the info I can find about EPO either says it hasn't been proved to do anything much, or is just waffly hippy crap that claims it cures Bad Energy etc. – if anybody has references to anything more balanced or more conclusive I'd be grateful.

janet mcknight

I did a search of Pubmed (http://www.pubmed.com) for 'evening primrose oil mastalgia' (mastalgia is the medical way of saying painful breasts) and got 19 results – you can read the abstracts of the papers there on the search engine. I hope that's helpful.

nb

In a word, yes! For me, evening primrose oil made my periods a heck of a lot less painful. So I continued to take it even after my breast pain had long gone. Well worth the minor pill-popping inconvenience in my book.

md

I had evening primrose oil recommended to me by friends for premenstrual depressions and I found it all made the whole thing much, much worse. I basically felt premenstrual for the whole month!

Some people I know swear by it, others had a similar reaction to me – whatever their particular PMT thing was, that's what they got all month long. Not at all related to your particular reaction, except to confirm that yes, EPO can affect your hormones and your cycle.

caroline

Shopping and Clothes

LUMPY BRA

Anyone got any tips on how to reshape padded bras once they come out of the washing machine before hanging out to dry? I'm sick of lumpy-looking breasts under tight-fitting tops!!

ebee

Maybe put something like a grapefruit in the cups while they are still damp. They should dry to fit, if you see what I mean. You could hang the bra up like a hammock (sorry, only word I could think of) so the weight of the fruit pulls the cups into shape.

cookwitch

You really should wash your bras by hand to preserve them. It doesn't take all that long; I wash mine in the sink while I'm bathing, then hang them up over the tub when I'm done.

lothie

I CAN WEAR SKIRTS!

Whoever it was suggested cutting off tights to wear under summer skirts to prevent thigh-chafing was TOTALLY spot on. Tried it yesterday and didn't feel much hotter than you would normally feel in the Lovely London Heat. Survived an evening at the pub. No chafing at all, no dilemma as to what I can wear today in order not to aggravate the results of yesterday's rubbing and pain. Try it!

- Take a cheap/old pair of tights
- Chop off the bottoms of the legs – I initially chopped them off to about knee length, but in the end took a couple of inches more off the bottoms so that they were about mid-thigh length.
- Wear! There so far doesn't appear to be any need to hem them or do anything about them running (although we'll see more when they've been washed).

Make sure it's a pair that fits properly in the first place. I don't know about anyone else on here, but the suffering caused by an ill-fitting pair of tights can be as bad as or even worse than the chafing itself.

sera_squeak

Bigger ladies can buy cut-off tights at Evans and they're hemmed, with reinforced crotch etc.

princesswannabe

FORMAL CLOTHEs

I'm absolutely sick of the hassle
of having to find outfits for
formal occasions – this evening
I'm going to a posh birthday do
where smart dress is required, and the weekend
after next I'm going to a wedding. Last year was
a nightmare, with five weddings.

I don't normally spend a lot on clothes, and I
really resent having to spend a lot of money on
things I'm only going to wear a couple of times
and don't *actually* like. What pisses me off the
most is that guys don't have this trauma – they
just buy one suit, a couple of shirts and ties and
that's it, they're sorted for every occasion for the
next ten years. I'm so tempted to just get a
neutral trouser suit and do the same. Just the
one. Not a light summer one, and a darker
winter one, and a shorter day one and a longer
evening one, and one that goes with those shoes,
and another that doesn't clash with that jacket,
one for work and one for play... AARGH!

I just hate this – every time an event comes up
it's an exercise in compromise between aes-
thetics, cost and hassle, and I really hate it.
Blokes don't appreciate quite how easy they've
got it.

dozle

Just get a nice skirt or trouser suit that's in a non-standard colour (and not green – you should never wear green to weddings, so says my mother) and a few nice tops that you can cycle through so it doesn't look obvious that you're wearing the same thing every time. And maybe dress it up with scarves, brooches, different jewellery and stuff..?

easternpromise

Seconded. A nice trouser suit can be dressed up with a fancy top and jewellery for the evening and a brooch on the jacket can make it look different for each wedding/event you attend. Don't be tempted to go for something completely utilitarian – it's not something that you'd want to wear to work (although maybe for posh Xmas dos) – splurge a little – after all, you're saving money on all the other outfits you won't be buying. And with a trouser suit you can wear flats or heels depending on how long you're going to be standing/walking/... which again will completely change the appearance of the outfit.

am

Have you had a look in Tesco or Asda for well-designed and very cheap outfits that can be dressed up with a wrap or jewellery? Having said that, I have a couple of made-to-measure four-piece suits for very formal stuff – highly recommended!

JJ

I have one smart dress with one set of smart shoes to match. I'm not into the smart thing, but it does

help that the dress is reasonably flattering on me. I'll
wear it to every wedding, work do or smart thingy
I have to go to, and don't care if anyone happens to
notice that it's the same outfit every time. If you
only have the one outfit but you look good in it,
why not wear the same thing for ten years? (Grin!)
But then, it does help that I don't go to that many
smart dos, and generally it's a different set of people
each time.

If you have to do the smart thing on a regular basis,
maybe just get two or three outfits and rotate them,
and aim for something you can reuse over several
years. Buying them is a pain – do you have a fashion-
savvy chum you can take shopping to help you pick
out something both flattering and timeless?

md

*I'm so tempted to just get a neutral trouser suit and do the
same.*

Then do that. I don't think people notice others'
clothes choices that much (especially if it's something
fairly timeless/neutral – if you wore, say, a gold
chainmail dress every time then yeah, it might be
remarked upon!). Also, if the bride, groom, other
guests, or anyone else looks adversely on your
clothing choice, then they're being crap and you
shouldn't worry about them. Spend the money on
stuff you actually like!

I have only been to two weddings in the last three
years, and can only remember what I wore to one of
them – but it was a dress I really liked, have worn
since, and I am pretty sure I didn't buy for the occasion. And it came from Camden, so not exactly
traditional formal (purple with pretty sequins on!). I

possess one pair of low-kitten-heel smart sandals, one pair of smart ankle boots, and that will do me fine.

jk

I think a mix-and-match suit is a great idea with a couple of different tops. Accessorising does sound like a nightmare, but if you get a couple of pieces that you keep with the outfit you can just sling them on whenever.

clare s

One multipurpose dress. A few pretty accessories. Sorted.

I have a black short-sleeved jersey dress which is smart enough to wear for weddings (with a colourful pashmina and matching hair-ties/earrings/whatever-I-can-be-bothered-with), could be worn for interviews with a jacket over it if I didn't have to cycle to them, and does for all the orchestra concerts I have to play in (black dress or black-skirt-and-white-blouse obligatory). It's empire-line, so it fits and still suits no matter what my waist size is doing (within reason). It machine-washes and doesn't need ironing. Got it from BHS about ten years ago for a tenner and it's one of the best buys ever.

It's so frustrating buying clothes in a hurry for a particular event and then not feeling happy with them and/or never wearing them again and feeling you've wasted the money; it's really, really worth finding something you're happy with that will do for lots of different things. On the other hand, if you really don't want to have to think about even one accessory, find a dress that fits/suits in a style you like that will do for lots of different occasions, and buy seven of them in different colours – just like blokes apparently do with their shirts! And black shoes go with everything, so no need to mess about thinking about shoes once you've got one pair you like.

janet mcknight

Buy a suit. I have a suit that I have worn to graduations, weddings, formal dinners, funerals, christenings, interviews and work things. It's black, I wear it for summer and winter dos, and all I have to decide is whether to wear a white T-shirt or a white shirt; black DMs or black boots; overcoat or not.

I'm trying to think how long I've had it. And I'm coming up with seven years and it still looks good. If you're going to get a suit, it's worth getting a good one. Mine was from Austen Reed.

k425

I work in a 'smart casual wear' office and have a couple of suits. So yes – I basically wear office stuff plus random jacket to weddings etc. Smart evenings – I have a lovely hip-length silver moire top that gets seen a lot, with whatever ends up underneath – usually a black work skirt/trousers.

Men may have it easy, but their suits are HUGELY expensive for a good one: £600 for hubbie's one good suit.

blue_cat

A good jacket and appropriately smart shoes are a great way of formalising any outfit, including pretty summer dresses. It is nice to just be able to reach into the wardrobe and pull out something appropriate that you don't have to think about.

gg

BRAS RIDING UP

What does it mean if your bra starts really riding up at the back? All of mine have started doing this over the past month or so, but when I measure myself I haven't changed size!

seren

I'd say it means you're wearing the wrong size. Has this always happened when wearing the particular size you take? Maybe measuring yourself is throwing out the sizing slightly? Might be worth going to a shop and getting measured, or trying on a few different sizes to see if they're any better?

easternpromise

It happens to me, I believe because the bra is old and has stretched/sagged. Try the next set of hooks in (if possible), otherwise go and get professionally measured and buy a nice crisp new bra.

blue_cat

That's exactly it. When you have a bra with too large a back measurement it rides up, but if the size you usually buy only fits on the tightest hooks, when the elastic stretches a bit it will ride up in the same way. So, buy bras that fit on the loosest set of hooks, then as the elastic fades you can move in through the hooks and save yourself buying new bras all the damn time. And remember that if you drop a back measurement you'll need to go up a cup size.

classytart

ANN SUMMERS – ORDERING ON THE INTERNET

Plain wrapping. Yay!
Ann Summers shows up on statement. Grrrr.
Automatic sub to the mailing list if you order by email. Grrrr.
Minus two points for Ms Summers

secretrebel

INTERVIEW SUITS

If all goes well I shall be applying for academic jobs within the next few months and hopefully having interviews for the same. I am therefore starting to look about for an interview suit, as I am chronically indecisive about such things and also very picky, and this is something I'd like to feel very happy and comfortable wearing.

Looking around appropriate shops, I find myself in something of a dilemma as regards what sort of suit to buy. I see some nice suits in striking colours (dark red, purple, green etc.) that would look good on me (I have the right complexion for such colours) but I'm not sure whether it would be good, bad or neutral for an interview suit to be that striking. I also see some nice suits in classic, muted colours but which have fun details – basically, classic with a twist, and, obviously, normal boring suits in black/ grey/pinstripe/etc.

What sort of suit do I want? What would make the best impression given the jobs I'll be applying for?

sk

I always interview in a coloured suit (figuring that even if they forget my name after a day of endless new faces they'll remember the woman in the pink/

purple/whatever colour suit!) and you've a lot more flexibility in academia anyway so I would say go for the fabulous striking colours.

The basic thing you should be looking for is something that makes you feel fabulous, confident and competent. I came down to London to interview for my current job and I was on the Tube in my pink suit surrounded by people in greys and blacks, and I felt like someone off Sex and the City (which is a good thing to me). I felt like a million dollars heading into that interview, and I have no doubt that it showed. Whether it got me the job I couldn't say, although it almost certainly made me more confident when doing the meet and greet at the beginning of the interview (something I hate).

caroline

Whatever suit you feel makes you saleable to the company. If you think the striking ones would stand out too much then you won't be certain about getting the job!

wyvernfriend

For academic jobs, I would say go for what you feel good in. I recently interviewed for, and was offered, a job as a graduate teaching assistant (low-level academic); I wore grey wide-legged trousers, purple mock-croc high-heeled boots (just visible under the trousers!), and a striped shirt (from Pink; lovely quality!) in various shades of grey, purple, lilac etc. I have blue/purple hair, so I tend to go for either fairly neutral or reasonably matching clothes, and so far have never had a problem in academia!

In general, I would say that an outfit should have one main striking detail: if the suit is a striking colour, go for a simple cut and wear it with a fairly neutral shirt or top. If you go for something with a 'twist', keep it a more neutral colour. If you go for a neutral, simple suit, dress it up with an interesting top or accessories (a nice scarf, an interesting brooch, for example). It's fine for your outfit to get you noticed, but obviously *you* want to stand out more than your clothes do!

sushidog

Remember first of all that hardly anybody on an interview panel has ever said, 'Well, she was clearly the best candidate, but I didn't like her suit!' Which is to say that wearing something you feel comfortable in is overwhelmingly the most important thing. If wearing a coloured suit will make you squirm and worry about looking too bright, then don't. If it'll make you feel like you look fine and allow you to concentrate on the things that you are saying, then coloured is excellent. Personally, I would go with coloured and just make sure that you wear it with a fairly simple (and coordinating) top underneath and simple jewellery. It might be different in a very formal environment – I believe that women are still advised to wear skirts rather than trousers to interviews in traditional law firms, though that might have changed over the last few years – but I really don't think it'll be a problem in academia. Make sure that whatever you are wearing will make you feel pleased with your appearance, and you'll be absolutely fine.

la bias

BOOTS

Having gotten my feet thoroughly soaked on the way home yesterday, I think it's about time I invested in a decent pair of boots. But which kind? I want a pair that'll last this time, not a cheap pair that'll 'do for now'. My requirements are: comfy for walking, flat soled, durable. I know Docs used to fit this category, but do they still have that reputation? Is there anything else I could try?

caturah

Docs are indeed good, but they do need a fairly significant amount of breaking-in before they're really comfortable. At least the veggie ones that I have did, but after three years they're holding up quite well, and I've only had to have them resoled once so far. Or you could get some steel-toed work-boots – they're VAT free!

t

Steel-toed work-boots – try the Army and Navy.

gg

The best pair of boots I've owned so far were by Ecco. My bf bought them for me for my 30th birthday and I was gutted when they ceased to be comfortable 12 years later. I replaced them with a pair by Rohde, which were fine for the first two winters, but my feet have grown slightly (combination of pregnancy and weight gain) and they don't fit me any more. I'm now saving for another Ecco pair.

kate atkin-wright

I swear by the company Hoggs, who make farmers' boots. For the past six years I've worn out about four pairs of their ankle boots. They are comfortable, don't take long to break in – soles with good grip – perfect for riding in – if you are into that (I have two horses, so my boots have to make do as riding boots). I wear mine all the time, every day and everywhere I go – including taking them to Spain with me!

There are two types, one heavier set that I usually get costs around £50, the other a lighter set which I just got, which are around £40.

I wouldn't buy any steel-toe-capped boots because they are COLD! Think about it – you've got a metal plate above your toes – that doesn't add warmth to your feet, instead it just sucks it away. Unless you have a reason to be wearing them, I wouldn't bother – and the only reason I consider valid is the likelihood of something heavy running over or stepping on your toe. They really aren't worth it. However, the boots I wear, I've worn everywhere – from working in a kennels, a stable, to being a shop assistant in Evans. I get mine from a farm supply store.

td

I have a pair of Hobbs' biker boots, which were horribly expensive. HOWEVER, they are turning out to be worth every penny of £150 and I love them madly. I wore them about every day last winter, from October to March, and they still look great and really smart. They're completely leather, so my feet never get too hot in them, even on days when the sun comes out. And they're great with both trousers and skirts.

Then a month ago one of the straps broke, so I took them back to the shop yesterday and said that I'd had them 11 months, but that since I'd paid £150 for them I felt the shop should pay for the repairs. They took one look at them and offered me a refund or replacement. So, realistically, it looks like I might be wearing them practically every day for four or five winters or more, which makes the £150 seem perfectly reasonable. Honestly, I can't rave about them enough. They're completely fantastic.

la bias

My Docs let in the wet on seriously bad days, due to the fact that the leather of the uppers has cracked where my foot bends at the toes (probably due to me not taking any care of them, mind you!). But in anything other than a real downpour they're still fine. (They're about three years old.)

Army boots are my real favourite, though – I got them through the Civil Defence when I was a member, but I believe places like Millets sell them. Insanely comfortable, utterly waterproof, take less time than Docs to break in, and they last well. I used to wear mine all day every day all year long, and they lasted five or six years before I finally wore through the soles.

dorian

VEGAN SHOES ADVICE

I just found Beyond Skin, who do posh vegan shoes. Thought it might be of interest to some: http://www.beyondskin.co.uk/html/home.php.

fgc

SUSPENDERS

How the arse do you attach suspenders to stockings?!

glassarmy

Ah yeah, they are tricky little buggers! The easiest way I find is to put the back bit under and hold on to it really tightly then place the other bit over and push the little button thing through and keep you finger on it and push it up the way, it took me ages to get the hang of it!

rebecca mcallister

The ribbons 'look pretty' (i.e. serve no purpose except to get in the way when trying to do them up).

Put – and hold tightly – the material over the button, then push the circle over the lot and slide the circle up and the button down... (there is a suggestion that once said stockings are 'connected' the ribbons supposedly lie over the top of the bump the suspenders produce and make it less visible... but it's a lie (and the ribbons never stay in place anyway).

vampwillow

I use the bits of ribbon to pull the connector over the button.

clare s

You really have to push: I use my thumb to try and shove it through.

I *think* the ribbons are just to cover the clips so they look prettier and don't rub your legs, or maybe they just put them there to piss you off and get in the way even more!

angel_virus

Old-fashioned suspenders were big enough to deal with woollen stockings, and my mother says that when the knob bit broke off they used to use a threepenny bit instead. Not that that helps you now, but now you know why God invented TIGHTS. (Which make me itch like crazy, but you can't have everything.)

ailbhe

Does the suspender belt have metal or plastic clasps? Plastic ones are basically useless. Metal ones are much easier to use and also stay attached.

kiss_me_quick

BUYING JEANS

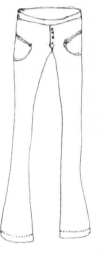

I like M&S jeans. They usually fit me perfectly (at 5ft 4in, with slightly longer than proportionate legs, I'm a regular). The last two years' ones were all George at Asda, though I went from an 18 postpartum down to a 12 and then back up again when I got pregnant. For £4 they are pretty darn good.

myf

Ooh, buying jeans is traumatic. I have a curvy figure (as in, my waist is quite a lot smaller than my hips) and I find it incredibly difficult to find jeans that fit me comfortably and don't reveal my underwear every time I sit or bend down! (If I want someone to see my undies, I will take him home and jump on him, thank you very much!) There used to be one particular make that were great, but they've stopped making them, so now I generally just go to lots of different places, try on lots of different pairs, and buy whichever fits me best; my favourites at the moment come from Dorothy Perkins and Debenhams. You may find it helpful to go to a jeans shop or concession so you can try on pairs by several different makers, as both sizes and shapes vary hugely!

sushidog

I am on a perennially low budget. I'm currently wearing jeans from New Look (tenner in the sale – bargain) which fit very nicely under the bum but are a bit baggy round the waist (enough to need a belt), but then I have a big under-bum and small waist. They are just the right thickness of material (can sit down in them but they still keep you warm) and quite long in the leg (I have long legs) and have a zip instead of silly fiddly buttons.

Also good: River Island black jeans that make thighs look ten times skinnier than they actually are, but quite tight around the bum. Again, a bargain tenner in the sale.

In my experience M&S use rubbish material for their jeans and the stitching is dodgy – the exact opposite quality of their bras. This may no longer be the case, but I'd steer clear as you don't generally get value for money (unlike the fab lingerie section, of course!)

Primark (don't laugh!) is also good for baggy comfortable jeans that last for ages, but fade pretty quickly in the sunlight. £8.

Tesco Jeans are only FOUR POUNDS MY GOD YES FOUR POUNDS, but often you can't try them on. The 14s are definitely too big for me but the trusty belt comes to the rescue. They are very loose and the material is a bit thin, but incredibly comfy and at FOUR POUNDS you can buy three pairs in all different sizes. No, I don't work for Tesco, ahem...

ks

My current pair of jeans are lovely and came from Next. I've also bought jeans from M&S before – fine, but the black faded a bit, and Land's End – but that's mail order.

lannie

Mango – they do hipsters that are on the high side and cover my belly (this from a woman who doesn't like to go out without things safely pulled up to her waist), plus they turn my size – ahem – into a respectable 14.

jj

Last autumn I had a once-in-a-lifetime (or at least once-until-my-credit-card-recovers) treat of going to Harvey Nichols for a personal shopping appointment. Jeans were one of the specific things on my agenda, since all previous pairs I'd had were of the roomy, came-up-to-my-armpits variety. I tried on 20–30 pairs under the gimlet eye of my personal shopper, and I have a butter-soft bootcut pair that makes me look taller and skinnier than I have in a while.

The jeans cost way, way more than I would normally spend, but the expert advice was definitely worth it – the whole point of the personal shopper is not to say, 'Those all look great! You should buy them!' but to pinpoint what looks good on you and teach you how to look for the right things. I would think that most department stores with a personal shopping service could provide someone to help you find the right jeans for you, but I was impressed with how professional the woman from Harvey Nichols was. (Plus, she was a little older than me, not tall, and not a whippet.)

easterbunny

Monsoon always works for my voluptuous hourglass figure (14–16 these days). Their sizes are regular and they have varying leg lengths.

offensive_mango

Matalan does bizarrely good ones and a load of designer ones all uber cheap...

ebee

BRA-STRAP SLIPPAGE

I've often joked with my friends that I need knobs on the tips of my shoulders. That way nothing could slip off! I wish it were that easy, but I think installing something from my local hardware store would... hurt.

This seems to leave me with a bit of a dilemma. How exactly do I keep bra straps – and anything else with a shoulder strap! – from slip-ping off? I've tried nearly everything I can think of: tightening the straps, loosening them, shiny new and dingy old bras. Even different sizes! Nothing seems to help.

For a while I thought of coating the underside of each strap with a flexible rubber coating – something like you find on strapless bras. I scoured the craft stores looking for such a beast, and I couldn't find a thing. This problem hasn't gotten any better with time. It's uncomfortable and embarrassing to put them back in place up to a dozen times a day.

Does anyone else have this problem? Does a solution exist?

tess flynn

Solutions exist. You can buy straps that run between your bra straps at the back to hold them closer to-gether (a brand-name is the Braza Strap-Mate). I think M&S used to sell a thing you could attach to your straps at the shoulder, like a pad to make them wider, which was possibly rubberised and was supposed to hold them on. Those probably exist somewhere still. There are also little clippy things you sew into the shoulders of your clothes, to attach straps to – less practical, but worth being aware of.

Or you could go for racer-back bras, or buy multi-way bras with detachable rubber straps, or use a multiway bra with one long strap in a halter-neck style...

JK

Make sure you're wearing the right size of bra! My straps stopped slipping off my shoulders so much when I started wearing the correct size. Measuring isn't always accurate! All the support should be coming from around the band, which should feel very tight, with the straps just there to add a little shape.

ceiswyn

WEDDINGS

My friend and I are differing on this. I feel that inviting a person to the ceremony and then the evening party is fine, but she believes it's better just to invite them to the evening party, not the ceremony. So if it was your invitation, would you be more insulted if you were asked to attend the wedding ceremony and the evening party (not the sit-down meal), or NOT the ceremony, just the evening party (not the sit-down meal), or other (please explain)?

meepettemu

I once went to a wedding where all my friends were invited to the sit-down meal and I wasn't – that was absolutely horrible. I went away and cried all afternoon.

If I'm one of a group who's not invited, or I don't

really know any of the other guests at all, it wouldn't bother me though – it can be fun to wander off and explore wherever the wedding is.

the_alchemist

If, for example, you are doing a meal for family only and cannot invite your friends, it would be good to include with the information you send them some details of places they could go in between – this is especially important for people who have travelled a long way.

jfk

The first option would be a bit confusing. Would they go to the ceremony, go home again, and then come out again for the party? Second option makes more sense!

teqkiller

You can't technically *not* invite someone to the cere-mony – if it's in England and Wales it has to be publicly accessible, so that anyone who might want to can announce they have 'just cause or reason why these two people cannot be joined...' Effectively you are just providing them with details.

mjf

We did not specifically invite people to the ceremony and evening reception but to just the evening recep-tion. What we did do was add a note to say if people wished come along to the wedding it was being held at such and such a church etc.

Personally, if I were invited specifically to both I

would feel obliged to go to both or neither. Really I would prefer to have the day to do stuff in, rather than being broken into bits.

clare s

I wouldn't be insulted by either option. As far as I'm aware, most couples tend to invite a select few to the ceremony and then stagger the arrival of others via dinner and the evening do. It's practical, and ensures you share the more important special moments with those you are closest to and then celebrate the event with everyone you care about.

ti

I'd be pleased to have any sort of invite. As long as I was staying overnight, I'd be happy for any combination, really. If it was a long way to get to, then I'd probably have to think hard about whether it would be better to go just for an evening thing, or whether to use the money the travelling etc. would cost to get a wedding present a bit more special. I'd be fine with ceremony and evening but not wedding breakfast, as above.

velvetpurrs

I wouldn't be offended by either, although in the first instance I would probably politely decline the invitation to the ceremony and just go to the evening party, unless the venue was very close by. (As I actually did earlier this year – the ceremony was in a fairly sizeable church, the sit-down meal venue was much smaller, and people were invited to the ceremony and for a drink in the pub over the road after, but we felt that just going to the evening do would be easier.)

Organising weddings is a nightmare. Someone will be offended whatever you do!

wh

I wouldn't be offended by either, although I think inviting people to the ceremony but not the sit-down meal is a tad odd.

If I received a wedding invitation from friends I'd be grateful and attend if I could. Weddings are logistical nightmares, you can't invite everyone to all of it (nor, frankly, would you want to); *shrugs* – what's to get offended about?

caroline

I wouldn't be insulted either way. The last thing I'd want to do would be to spoil a friend's special day by getting in a snit about not being invited to their party. It's a privilege to be invited to any of it at all!

janet mcknight

WEDDING LISTS

Having, after many sagas with them, decided against John Lewis for the wedding list, I'm now very tempted by

WrapIt. Has anyone had any good/bad experiences with them?

fgc

When using them for a friend's wedding I found their agents quite pushy on the phone (beware if you have a dear old aunt Gladys who will phone rather than use the internet) and they had to wait some time after the wedding before gifts were sent out. They do have some beautiful items, but it might be worth having a backup list or just gift vouchers with Debenhams/John Lewis/House of Fraser or whatever for people who like a simple life.

r.a-b

Hate hate hate them – best mates used them for their wedding in October, and they're still trying to sort out presents that were damaged or just plain wrong.

ti

MUM PRESENTS

My mum turns 50 very soon and I want to be able to get her something special. I don't know what to get, I have been racking my brain and everything seems too clichéd or too over the top.

My mum won't let us make a big fuss, no parties etc. We will probably get away with taking her out for a meal. She also doesn't want to go for days out or an 'experience'. She can't use bubble bath or the like as it triggers thrush.

I've got a budget of about £50 but can go up to £100 for something really good. My brother has the same budget and we can easily pool resources and get something together.

Has any one got any ideas? I really love my mum and want to get her something fab.

tooth_fairy

Something she'll wear, perhaps? A brooch for a jacket lapel? a silk scarf or shawl? a dress ring? a necklace and earring set for nights out?

nicky s

Theatre tickets?

vicky l

If she hasn't got a digital camera, how about one? If you got one with a printer, that might be good. I'm older than your mum, but my camera means the world to me. Honestly, I get so much from mine – not just family photos, but trying out arty ones, I sent four to BBC Digital Britain. I was so chuffed to see them there!

aellia

Has she got a garden? I bought my brother a willow tree for his 40th which he loves. I think there's a website that will actually deliver – can't remember the URL off the top of my head but it's something like treesdirect.co.uk.

cazmanian minx

Health

THRUSH

Three tablespoons bicarbonate of soda in a warm bath plus a few drops of either Tea Tree or lavender oil works wonders when you have thrush.

cookwitch

SOOTHING INSECT BITES

To soothe and help an insect bite heal faster, dab some plain peppermint toothpaste on it and leave to dry (use the white stuff, not the blue gel type). The mint soothes and cools and helps stop the itching, as well as helping dry it out and heal.

velvetpurrs

This works on spots too.

lucrezia borgia

ATHLETE'S FOOT

Soaking your feet in warm water with a splodge (technical term, that) of vinegar will treat athlete's foot better than anything I've ever bought from a chemist.

alt

RESTLESS LEGS

Stupid as it may sound, it's a real diagnosable thing. It's actually called restless legs syndrome. My flatmate has it in spades – she could kick your eye out at 15 paces when she's tired. The advice she was given was to take more calcium and magnesium (CalMag tablets), and it really really helps.

syleth

I've been getting it for the last few months, during pregnancy, and was told by my GP that it's due to too much salt and too little potassium. She recommended a glass of milk and a banana about an hour before bed time – it seems to work. I'll sometimes go for a quick walk around the block with the dogs too if I'm feeling really twitchy.

mn

My husband has started eating sunflower seeds, and the almost nightly cramps seem to have disappeared.

gemma

I used to wake up screaming with calf cramps, and I was told to drink tonic water with quinine in it.

sd

LACTOSE INTOLERANCE

My partner is lactose intolerant and she keeps a bottle of lactase enzyme in the fridge for when she goes to a restaurant etc. It doesn't eliminate the problem, but it makes it a lot more tolerable.

auntysarah

HERBAL TRANQUIL- LISERS

I use valerian tincture. I'm not one for pills, because there are something like 200 active parts to the plant and in making the pills they just extract the part they feel is the most useful. IMO, to get the most out of it you should take the whole product. Valerian tincture (or just the herb) has the added value of being a cat drug too. It's like catnip, only better. The downside is that it tastes like strong cheese/manky socks.

meepettemu

I love Kalms, totally recommend them... been using them on and off for about 15 years now (eek!). They do seem to calm me down – insomnia, job stress, relationship stress, exams... everything. And you can get them in REALLY big jars.

suzylou

ANTIBIOTICS

Eat plain, live yoghurt when taking antibiotics as it helps stop thrush and/or upset stomach.

cookwitch

COUGHING

I have a tickly cough. This is somewhat worrying, because I'm a singer and have a really important concert on Sunday that I desperately don't want to miss. Singing itself isn't such a problem – it's keeping from coughing while on the platform.

Today I'm working from home so I don't have to use my voice at all. And sucking Halls Soothers constantly. My singing teacher says that every time I want to cough I should drink water and try to swallow instead.

Will consider all and any other suggestions – particularly from other singers?

westernind

In a cup of hot water, dissolve one heaped teaspoon of honey and one tablespoon of apple cider vinegar. Use boiling water, and while it's still too hot to drink, inhale the fumes.

caturah

As a singer, I would say that Vocalzone are the dog's b*llocks and I'm never without them. For some reason you don't get them in Superdrug. It has to be Boots, or an independent chemist... And I actually quite like the taste of them!

pipistrellus

SLIMMING PILLS – ADVICE

Slimming tablets fall into various categories. There are some which are essentially very close to amphetamines: they 'work' by suppressing your appetite and making you restless, so you feel like crap and you eat very badly. Yes, you might lose some weight, because you're essentially starving yourself, but as soon as you stop taking the pills your appetite will return, you'll eat properly again, and it'll take at least a few days if not weeks for your body to come out of fat-storing starvation mode, so you'll pile on any weight you lost and probably add some more for good measure.

Then there's the ones that prevent you from digesting fat properly. Now, obviously, if you eat fat and can't digest it, it has to go somewhere, which means these ones give you fatty diarrhoea. Lovely. They also deprive your body of 'good' fats, so your skin dries out, and you're deprived of useful nutrients like vitamin E.

Then there's the possibly apocryphal tapeworm-egg tablets. These do what they (usually don't) say on the tin: they contain tapeworm eggs. Allegedly they come with a second tablet that you take when you've lost enough weight, which is supposed to kill the tapeworm. Problem is, tapeworms can reproduce in your stomach, and their eggs can pass into the bloodstream and then lodge in other places in your body. Have I put you off these sufficiently yet? Good.

The 'safest' sort are the bulk pills, the sort where you're supposed to take ten or 20 a day; they usually consist largely of cellulose (plant fibre) which is indigestible, so they fill you up and stop you feeling hungry without adding calories. You'll probably feel bloated and icky, and they may give you either constipation or diarrhoea (depending on exactly what's in them), and again, they essentially encourage you to starve yourself, so you lose weight, and then once you start eating properly again you put it all back on.

Basically, there is no quick fix to weight loss except hacking off a limb or two. If you want to lose weight, you need to change your eating habits and your exercise habits. Don't diet: diets don't work. You need *long-term* change, because short-term changes give you short-term effects only. The simple equation is that if calories burnt > calories absorbed, you lose weight. If calories burnt < calories absorbed, you put on weight.

Try thinking about what you eat on a daily basis. Do you eat breakfast? If not, start now. Go for something high-fibre, like porridge, which will give you energy throughout the morning and discourage you from snacking. If that doesn't work, try having something high-protein and low-fat in the morning; some people find that fills them up better than high-fibre.

Do you snack? If so, what do you snack on? Try replacing your snacks with fresh or dried fruit and veg instead of crisps or biscuits or chocolate.

Do you tend to eat fatty things? Or processed food? Go for low-fat choices, which are not processed. Make sure you eat at least five portions of fruit and veg every day, and drink two litres of water; if nothing else, that will fill you up a bit, and thus discourage you from eating junk.

Whatever you eat, ask yourself whether it is 'useful' food, or nutritionally empty. If it has fresh fruit and veg in it, then that can excuse *some* fat/processed carbs etc. But if you're eating, say, a Big Mac, there's almost no nutrition in it at all and a lot of fat, salt and additives. It is 'empty' food, and it's a waste of a meal.

sushidog

CHIRO-PRACTORS

Has anyone here ever been treated by a chiropractor? I have a terrible pain in my back with shooting pains going down my leg and pain in my hip. We have a couple of chiropractors

locally and I want to know if they are likely to be able to help me (and, importantly, how much it will cost).

zoefruitcake

Does it run down the back of your leg? If it does, that might be sciatica, which is a nerve problem, so I'm not sure if a chiropractor would help much. Chinese massage and acupuncture sorted me out when I had it.

cookwitch

My personal experience has been that chiropractors can fix the immediate problem but you have to keep going back to them quite frequently (when I used to see a chiro it was once every six weeks or so). An osteopath, on the other hand, can do a proper fix, which may require two or three visits to get totally sorted, but when it's done it's done.

vicky l

As I understand it, chiropractors tend more to lots of little movements, whereas osteopaths do Large Fixing Things, although I could be wrong. I haven't had chiropractic but have been to osteopaths (in my case unfortunately it's not just a single fix – basically, my desk-based job does not make my back happy, so the fixes only last for about six months at a time). I would recommend it for back pain – a decent osteopath should be able to tell if it's something they can fix (e.g. trapped nerve or similar) or something else.

No use to you, sadly, as you're not London-based, but in case anyone else is interested, the British School of Osteopathy has cheap appointments available – you're seen by a third- or fourth-year student, with a tutor supervising. I've had excellent treatment there.

jk

My mum and I have had miraculous results from osteopaths – instant fixes from crippling pain that went on for months before treatment.

Bear in mind that not all osteopaths use exactly the same techniques. I had been suffering crippling pain in my neck, face and head. On my first session I had one bloke where, although the treatment was soothing, I was still plagued by the pain afterwards.

On my second session, same practice, different bloke, radically different technique, the pain was fixed instantly. I felt the exact moment it clicked away. Fantastic.

So basically, you may have to shop around if it doesn't work straight away. When you're in pain, you may as well try everything going (I tried acupuncture but it did nothing for me). Personally though, I'd start with a couple of osteopaths and move on to a chiropractor if you have no luck.

md

HEADLICE

Washing hair in vinegar is as good (sometimes better) a method of getting rid of head lice as the shampoos etc. that you buy over the counter at the chemist.

silvernik

AROMA-  THERAPY

I've been thinking about exploring homeopathy and aromatherapy to see how they could help my various conditions. Can anyone recommend any good comprehensive books on both or either subject? Thanks!

loulou

Valerie Worwood's *The Fragrant Pharmacy* is my aromatherapy bible. She's really excellent, comprehensive, well written and clear.

gg

FOOD ADDIC- TION

How can you tell if you have a food addiction? Ever since puberty I've been obsessed about food and weight. If I wasn't planning my next meal I was always planning on how to avoid food, yet somehow it always involved food. As a teenager I was bulimic, but I got over that with a combination of exercise and love! However, I am still always thinking about food or how to avoid it, and it seems food has the ability to instantly make me happy or cheer me up, giving me 'something to look forward to'. As a result I will keep on shovelling food in, even if I am full, because I feel almost forlorn when I am out of food.

I don't know how this happened, but of course it has resulted in a weight battle. I am not fat or overweight, but I know it could happen very easily if I didn't watch myself. I was just wondering whether if this *was* a disorder some sort of help (where would I get it?) might help control my eating. I have no illusions about how awful this would be, though, because it's not like I can ever stop eating and so get away from the addiction.

siren

It's probably worth getting some counselling or similar help to try to disconnect the food from the happiness. Having to eat whenever you're miserable isn't healthy, as you've found, and a professional could help you disassociate the two and find other ways to lift your mood.

lfk

My version of this is that it is a psychological thing. I associate some (okay, a lot of) foods with a happy time, and so I am happy when I am eating them. My brain is associating them with the feeling of happiness I have. This is probably why, when my boyfriend is away, if I'm not careful I do things like eat a whole battenburg cake, and then dinner, and then drink a whole load of beer.

Yes, I'm worried about myself; and I'm afraid I don't have any answers for you. But I just wanted you to know it wasn't just you.

bee

I think that associating food with happiness, and eating to cheer yourself up, is quite common in women (not saying it's a good thing, just that you're not alone).

sd

SURGERY UNDER GENERAL ANAES-THETIC - WHAT TO EXPECT

I had a laparoscopic sterilisation last year, so I hope this helps give you some idea of what to expect. Obviously, things might be slightly different in your case.

Just beforehand I was given paracetamol, so that it had kicked in properly when I woke up. Then you go down to the prep room and the anaesthetist will swab the back of your hand to clean/numb it and then they inject it with anaesthetic. They might ask you to count or otherwise talk to them, and you won't get very far before you're asleep. I can't speak for anyone else, but I found it to be a really nice relaxing feeling.

You don't feel the passing of time when anaesthetised (like you do when ordinarily asleep), so you'll be woken up (what feels like) seconds later. Your abdomen might feel a bit tender, but at this point they will provide more painkillers if you need them. It won't take long for you to come round properly, but you might feel a bit sleepy for a while. After a bit they will bring you tea and toast (or something) to check you can keep solids/liquids down, and then assuming everything is OK you'll be free to go. I was out and on my way home about two to three hours after the op. They won't let you go if you're alone, so you'll need to have someone come and pick you up.

With the sterilisation I had two tiny incisions, one just above the pubic bone and one in my navel. I can honestly say I didn't feel the lower cut at all. I don't even remember it being tender, never mind painful. The higher cut was tender for a day or so, but after that it was completely fine. The hospital gave me painkillers to take at home, and they're still all sat here in the box because I didn't have any reason to take them. I was back at work two days later and felt completely fine.

Beforehand I worked myself up into a complete lather because I'd never been cut into (I had been under anaesthetic before) and yet afterwards I kicked myself for getting so worried about, well, virtually nothing. I'm not saying don't be nervous, because I know I was, but it will be OK and not even nearly as bad as you're imagining.

alt

REMEDIES FOR COLD SORES

I use the antiviral cream Zovirax (or Boots own brand version). As advertised, it's best if you can do it when you feel the tingling, but it still works pretty well on the full-blown cold sore.

Prior to that being invented I tried loads of different things, including perfume (ow ow ow ow ow. But it did dry it out and seemed to clear it up quicker), Blisteze cream (ammonia based, pretty much dissolves the scab. I still use this occasionally) and lip balm (softens it and stops it cracking and bleeding).

Cold sores are horrible. You have to be so careful about washing your hands all the time. And you don't get a snog for a week!

darth tigger

My dentist friend told me to just use Vaseline as Zovirax doesn't work any quicker once the cold sore's developed.

anna

Hold ice on it until it hurts. Seriously.

cartographer

Seconded with the ice thing. Other things that work are: a wet teabag (this was in *New Scientist*!); and I always take an amino acid called l-lycine, which seems to zap it quite quickly. Oh, and alas, stopping chocolate for the duration, as it has in it something that makes the cold sore worse (also read in *New Scientist*).

bee

Blistex relief cream (used to be called Blisteze) – stings like hell if it goes on an open wound, but it seems to dry them out to get them to the 'scab' stage faster, and help with healing.

Only used Zovirax the once – I think I was allergic to it, since it basically felt like it was dissolving the skin (although in retrospect that could have just been the blisters getting rubbed and opening up).

Zinc supplements taken regularly are supposed to help avoid them by boosting the immune system, but I always forget this till I get one! Mind you, I only get them when stressed, so avoiding stress is probably also a good pre-emptive cure.

sea_of_flame

BACK/BOOB PAIN ADVICE

If you get back pain because of the weight of your boobs, it may be worth trying to strengthen your core muscles (abs and lower back). Standard crunches will go a long way to strengthening the abs, but have you tried back bends to strengthen your lower back? Just lie on the floor on your tummy, put your hands by the side of your head and 'crunch' the muscles of your lower back to lift your chin and chest off the ground (slowly and in controlled fashion of course, otherwise it just hurts!) then rinse and repeat! It looks weird, but it's brilliant for your posture.

easternpromise

ALTERNATIVE MEDICINE

I wanted to ask a general question: how do you ladies feel in general about alternative medicine? Are you in favour? Cautious? Sceptical? Have people had much experience with alternative medicine?

My experience is limited: I've had homeopathic treatment twice. The first time I was about 10 or 11; I used to get horrendous colds and sinus infections when I was a kid, and my mother was told that I would grow out of it eventually but that nothing could be done in the meantime. This was not good enough, as quite often I had to sleep propped up on half a dozen pillows in order to be able to breathe. She took

me to a practitioner who used to be a GP but had become a bit disillusioned with mainstream medicine and was now working as a holistic practitioner. She asked me lots of questions, then fed me something that resembled non-minty tic-tacs or something. She said I'd get a really bad cold for a couple of days and then the problem would go away, which is exactly what happened. I still have no idea what it was she gave me.

My second lot of homeopathic treatment was less effective: while at university I started sleeping very badly (probably stress-related), and my doctor (who was evil anyway) basically refused me any help. I found a homeopathist, who asked me questions and gave me some stuff (don't remember what; this was almost a decade ago!). It didn't help me sleep, but it did trigger an allergic reaction – not to the stuff he gave me but to nickel; I still can't wear most metallic jewellery now, as it gives me contact dermatitis, which had never been the case before. Most odd.

Anyway, I'm now fairly sceptical about a lot of alternative medicine – the whole 'dilution to the nth degree' bit of homeopathy is just nonsensical, although mainstream medicine does use a fair amount of 'like with like' treatments (digitalis, for example). A lot of treatments seem to have fairly dire consequences in some cases (for example see the stuff on people who have been turned grey by taking colloidal silver!), and many of them have no basis of evidence that they actually work. Worse than that, it does seem that some of the people practising them are charlatans who are out for money and don't

really care about the people they're exploiting. In the case of mainstream medicine, treatments have at least been clinically tested, and with the NHS there's less likelihood of a doctor pushing expensive treatments in order to make a profit.

sushidog

I think alternative medicine and conventional medicine can complement each other very well. I personally have a fear of ending up taking too many drugs (even taking contraceptive and vitamins on the same day pushes that a bit).

I agree with you about homeopathy as it has no basis in conventional science, but at the same time, I've taken it before and it has worked, so I put that down to placebo effect in my mind.

I've also had reflexology, which worked wonders for my anxiety attacks when I was a child, and some Chinese herbs, which worked wonders for a bout of IBS I had before Xmas (even if I was sceptical of the terminology that was being used to describe what was wrong with me). So basically, I like to keep an open mind.

caturah

I think that 'conventional' medicine was the alternative once, so I'm willing to try anything.

zoefruitcake

I use Bach Flower Remedies – didn't think they'd work at all but I do notice the difference when I stop taking them now – and acupuncture, reflexology and reiki, all of which have worked wonders for me. I do have a fairly open mind about things though.

cookwitch

I swear by homeopathy. It's worked too well on me and my family for me not to think it works. It does kind of go against my scientific mind, but I've seen it work too often and too well. We use it to treat our son for teething, fevers, wind, colic etc., rather than dope him up with horrible baby medication full of aspartame and colourings. DH used it to treat me after my son's birth when I was completely fucked up (for want of a better phrase). It worked on me when I didn't even know what I was taking, and on occasions when I thought I was taking a completely different remedy.

Reflexology and acupuncture I've never tried, but I'd be happy to give them a shot.

sa

In times of extreme pain and desperation I've tried acupuncture and homeopathy, but I have to say, neither of them had the slightest effect. I did turn up to a reflexologist by mistake: I had terrible pain in my face and neck (the doctor had been no help at all) and I'd gone to this woman because I'd been told she did massage. No, not massage, reflexology. It sounded like utter bollocks to me, but I was too embarrassed to walk out and thought I might as well have one treatment (I was utterly convinced it would do nothing for my pain).

Er... it actually worked – an inverse placebo effect? I've no idea. I've used it a couple of times since then for pain. It seems to work for me.

md

My family use alternative therapies, mainly because the medical profession as a whole has treated us badly/ given us the brush-off/told us that having a label for our illnesses was pointless etc. etc. When you've been treated like that, and feel you've been hitting at a brick wall for so long, it sometimes feels as though you have no alternative, you know? My mother took me for acupuncture when I was about 6, as a way of hopefully avoiding having an operation. I wasn't a very suggestible child, so I don't think it was that, but the operation was avoided.

Middle brother is brain damaged and was given homeopathic treatments when very young, and just thought they were sweets. Results were very sudden and very noticeable. Homeo- pathic remedies don't work for me.

My mother has been extremely ill for a long time, and uses her various alternative therapies to get her through the day. I am more sceptical about many of them than she is, but she takes them and feels better for a lot of them, not worse.

My father has always been very sceptical and dis- missive of AT, to the point of being very down on my mother – until he developed arthritis, and now he's taking everything he can find an article on, and is feeling better.

bee

I am a big fan of complementary therapies and I do think they can be used to great effect. I would shy away from ANYTHING that suggested you should forgo conventional medications in order to take it.

Just my thoughts on the ones I have tried out:

- Western herbalism – this is pretty good, to be honest. I have in the past taken agnus castus for my cycle (as directed) and it does seem to have a positive effect. Negative points for it tasting really bad.
- Reflexology – did nothing for my underlying problems but I did feel good afterwards. So chilled out – I reckon a great stress buster.
- Reiki – not my scene, did nothing for me at all.
- Acupuncture – still having this and it's pretty good. I made DH go and he went reluctantly at first, but now he is very keen on it. I like it because it works well with conventional treatment. I am not seeing a therapist linked to herbal medicine as I do not want to take anything like that.
- Hair analysis and vitamin stuff – expensive, complex, with OK results.

Even if it is a placebo effect I think the mere act of doing something positive to help yourself and your situation is a boost

clare s

I'm all for conventional medicine – it saved me after all. I suffered from cancer and chemo helped. However, sometimes it just seems to be a sledgehammer to kill a fly, and often doctors doesn't seem to see the body as a system but just as individual symptoms, which makes no sense to me.

Some alternative therapists seem to be dangerously single-minded against conventional medicine, to the point of not telling people to move on to conventional medicine when their therapy fails.

My mother keeps pointing out that in an article in the *Irish Times* every Tuesday they interview medicos and ask them about alternative therapy and whether they use it, and most of them say no.

I've tried homeopathy (no real result), aromatherapy (nice massage and some of the oils quite useful for various things), reflexology (she told me stuff about my health I hadn't told her). I also found that, surprisingly, acupuncture seemed to help get me into a more balanced state of health, and I'm planning to go back again!

wyvernfriend

I'm also fairly sceptical, which is why when I'm thinking about using something I do some research on the web first – not basic websites, but the kind that say 'this is the research we did and here are the results'.

As well as the *New Scientist*, there's a chap who writes in the *Guardian*, Edzard Ernst, who holds the only Chair in complementary medicine in the UK and is a firm believer in rigorous scientific testing to see what does work and what is quack. And when he finds things that work, he wants research into how and why too. He's a good read. Tuesdays, in G2.

k425

EXERCISE VIDEOS

Recommend me a good exercise video!

vf

Lynne Robinson's 'Everyday Pilates' with Fern Britton is my favourite. Oh, and avoid 'Goddess Workout: Introduction to Bellydance'. It's truly awful and embarrassing to watch.

loulou

Louise Solomon's Yogalates.

tooth_fairy

If you want muscle toning rather than aerobic exercise then the two New York City Ballet DVDs are superb. They're brilliant and really work. They're not easy by any means (nothing that actually works ever is) but I really enjoy them.

caroline

My personal favourite is the 'Kylie Minogue Hot Pants' workout – it's Kylie's trainer rather than Kylie herself in it though, and don't try and do it on a carpeted floor, you need to be able to slide your feet.

cazmanian minx

If you want something short but hard work try any of the tae-bo ones. They might be short but you definitely work up a sweat, and it doesn't require as much coordination as aerobics.

ad

'Power Yoga' with Anne Marie. If you want something to make you fit and burn calories, Anne Marie's stuff is fiendishly hard. (Don't ever think yoga is a soft option – this one is certainly isn't!) I don't know what you're after, a gentle workout or a hard and sweaty one? This is a hard one. (Possibly tricky if you've never done any yoga before – don't end up snapping anything!) Quality of the vid is naff, but the best workout I've found so far.

md

The Carmen Electra strip aerobics ones are good for a laugh. I'll never look at ballet exercises in the same way again... The DVDs are quite short; I think you're supposed to repeat all the routines several times though.

sd

UPPER ARM EXERCISES

Hope I describe this well.

Sit on the edge of your bed, or a low chair. Slowly ease your bum off the bed, but hold on to the edge of the bed with your hands. Move your feet away from the bed as necessary to maintain comfort. With your weight supported by your arms, slowly raise and lower yourself repeatedly, like a reverse press-up.

Also, weights required for this one – for reference, the correct weight to use is one that is heavy enough to only allow you a certain number of repeats, no extra lifts. If you can do extra, you need a heavier weight. Hold your hands straight above your head, with a weight supported between them. Bend your arms at the elbow and lower the weight behind your head. Lift arms fully upright again. Repeat.

caturah

The best thing is slow, controlled work with hand weights. You can get decent hand weights for about £6 I think in John Lewis: get the heaviest you can manage and do a small number of repeats (8-12 one side, 8-12 t'other, and another set if you can manage it. To the point of fatigue, but not pain). Also, do the exercises every other day as the real effect comes from the muscles repairing themselves on a rest day.

anwen

Lifting weights will tighten the muscles but the fat won't go completely without some form of cardiovascular exercise. Basically fat-burning fitness training. Weights do burn a small percentage of fat, but they are mostly about training muscles to get leaner and more toned. The more toned they are the more fat they eat away. At the end of the day, though, toning exercises won't get rid of the fat that sits on top of muscles very well; you need to think about running, or cross-training or any other activity that speeds up your heart rate.

I was starting to get bingo wings, but they've gone just with running for 40 minutes per day. Just remember that flabby arms are caused by loose muscle and extra fat, so with a combination of toning/weight lifting you will tighten the muscle and cardio will burn excess fat.

siren

I recently started doing light weights for my arms. Just a couple of pounds, hold your arms out straight and pull into your chest as well as straight up and down. They're a little tighter and lighter now.

liese

For your triceps (backs of your upper arms) bring your elbows up behind you with your fists or hand weights close to your side below your armpits. Stretch your arms out backwards and then back again (like backwards bicep curls). Keep your elbows high!

gemma

SLIMMING WORLD AND TAI CHI

Anyone done these? Were they any good? Did it last? I'm looking to lose weight, get fitter and more relaxed. So I'm looking at my options. Any help/info gratefully received.

jules

My mum did Slimming World and it really worked for her because you can have unlimited amounts of certain foods – pasta, potatoes, rice and pulses on a green day, and unlimited lean meat and fish on a red day. She started around late August last year and has lost two stone and is now at her target; that happened around March/April I think. She's found it easy to stick to the diet, plus adding more treats now she's at her target, and has kept going to meetings free of charge now she's maintaining, so that she doesn't slip up and put the weight back on.

laura

I was on WeightWatchers last year, lost a stone and a half in four months, and it's stayed off.

cazmanian minx

Tai Chi is great. Haven't done it in a while, but it was V V good for fitness and raising energy levels.

mt

I didn't get on at all with Slimming World – I lost weight to start with, and then just started piling the pounds back on, even though I was sticking to the diet resolutely. In the end, the only way I could lose weight on Slimming World was to calorie count at the same time, which totally defeated the point of the diet! On the other hand, not every diet works for everyone, so the best thing is just try it and see if it works. If not, move on to the next diet. I've lost about four and a half stone in the last ten months on Weight Watchers, but it's not working so well for me at the moment so I'm considering switching to the GI diet.

As for Tai Chi, I think it really depends on what type you're doing. If it's just Form, then it won't do anything at all for your fitness levels. If you do Martial and Form, then you'll see improved fitness. If you want to work fitness, strength and flexibility, any martial art is good – I can especially recommend kickboxing; one of my (admittedly male) friends would highly recommend kung fu. The important thing, again, is to find something that works for you, and most especially something with a good teacher. You'll find the more inspiring your teacher the harder you'll work!

easternpromise

I do Body Combat and I love it – I've been doing it for three/four weeks now, and I'm slimmer and fitter! Body Pump is also good, but Combat is fantastic!

red_panda_bear

If you're not sure about which diet to do, a good idea is to research a couple of them and then ask your GP which they would recommend. I think the British Heart Foundation also produces a diet booklet of some variety, and Judith Wills has produced a couple of diet books which may have some merit (her low-fat cookery books are fantastic – you wouldn't even know you were eating low-fat food!).

Yoga is brilliant for ironing out all those lumpy bumpy bits! Ashtanga and Hatha are very good – I think Hatha tends to work the fitness levels a bit more than Ashtanga, but that's just a personal feeling.

Going back to the martial arts thing – try and get a recommendation for a local dojo from a friend or acquaintance. And go along and see if you can watch a class before trying it out. That'll give you an idea what their teaching methods are like, what sort of stuff they do in the class, and whether you'd get on with that. Be prepared to try three or four different arts until you find what you're looking for.

Remember the MMAs (modern martial arts – things like Jeet Kune Do, for example) tend to have less philosophy and a more eclectic style, whereas the traditional arts have a great deal of philosophy and lifestyle behind them, their own individual forms/kata, and an emphasis on a set number of techniques. Other arts, like kickboxing, are straight fighting arts with no philosophy or forms/kata behind them. It totally depends on what you're looking for.

easternpromise

I've done Tai Chi for more than six years now and I love it. For me it has the right balance of being challenging to learn, relaxing and fun, plus I get on really well with the people in the class. It has improved my balance in a way I would never have imagined. Good for general fitness and feeling healthier too.

My instructor is keen to teach the more martial aspects, which I think is good, unless you want the more 'hand-wavy' side. Ask them what forms they teach – apparently Sun style is quicker to learn, as is Yang style (although I found that hard). Chang Man Ching is the main style I do, and it's a good combination of posey/martial/fun.

Go to a couple of lessons and see whether you like it – you should be able to just pay for the first couple on the day, instead of booking a block.

nb

A diet will almost certainly make you more neurotic about food than you were when you started it, and also ingrain bad habits that will cause you to put on weight once you stop dieting. Physical exercise is a far better way to get healthy, if you can stand the tedium. Learning to eat healthily also helps.

sesquipedality

I did Slimming World a couple of years ago. I lost 21 lb in five weeks, but I lost interest; I have no will power and two years later have put the weight back on and more. The only thing stopping me going back to Slimming World at the moment is lack of money!

phoenix 1979

I lost five stone in ten months on the Slimming World plan. It works for me, and I even lost weight over Christmas. It's easy to stick to unless you get the urge for a ton of chocolate (which happens to me every now and then). You can eat lots and don't need ever to be hungry.

kate atkin-wright

STOMACH TONING

Do any of you know of any exercises I could do from the comfort (and privacy) of my own home that will help me lose weight and also tone my stomach at the same time?

lp

Pilates is good for strengthening all your lumbar muscles (those around your middle). Also, sit ups/ stomach crunches.

A rowing machine might be a decent investment – it's good for cardiovascular exercise, upper arms, legs, lumbar region... just about everything really. You can get decent ones for just short of £100 from Argos.

sara

There's also a lot of Pilates and yoga vids to do at home, I have a Lynne Robinson one which is great.

laumiere

If you get an abdominal exerciser then you can gently work on your stomach muscles – (I use one affectionately named by me the curly crunch, as that's pretty much what you do. Tiny little crunches – far less damaging than proper sit-ups and you can do lots of different ones). Remember, little and often is better than lots infrequently. Also, whatever you do don't do them within an hour (preferably two) of eating – it'll hurt.

Expect cramp-like sensations the day after the first few sessions as the muscles get used to being used again. These will pass as they strengthen.

You can also tighten tummy (and other) muscles whilst sat at your desk/in the car/pub/whenever you think. Just tense and release as many times as you like, as often as you like. It all helps.

With regard to the gym, a lot of gyms offer a quiet room for shy people, alternative times, classes and other forms of support. There may be a women-only gym near you too. OK, so the people working in the gym will all be fit because that's what they do all day, but trust me, most of the people in there will be there for the same reason as you, and unless you pick a really posey one (and go look at a few before you select) then the vast majority of people cannot see past the sweat in their own eyes.

am

For toning stomachs, my mother always says stomach crunches – lying on the floor with your knees bent and hands by your ears and trying to touch your knees with your elbows. Although I keep reading that this can be bad for your neck, and then other articles saying it's not. So who knows?

notcollins

I'm in a similar position. I didn't think there were any specific exercises that would help – the muscles themselves are probably fine (although toning them further wouldn't *hurt*), but the problem is a layer of fat and excess skin ABOVE the muscles, which ain't going to be touched by sitiups and whatnot.

As far as I know, the only answer is to wear a tummy minimiser thingie and/or get a tummy-tuck. I already do the former and I'm actually seriously considering the latter once I'm certain I've had all the babies I'm going to have!

vicky l

GIVING BLOOD

It's the first time I'll have ever done it, so I'm a little bit nervous – not really worried about the process, at least not in my head (I've had lots of blood tests before, and I've had an IV drip, so I know it's all reasonable stuff that my body can cope with), but more about whether I'll faint. I

did faint once after a blood test (though I was really tired and ill at the time), but every other time I've been fine so long as I get to lie down (which presumably you do for giving blood – yes?).

The thing is, my boyfriend (who has given blood about a million times and is awfully smug about it) says that if you even hint to them beforehand that you're worried about fainting they will refuse to let you give blood at all, because they can't take the risk. This sounds a bit screwy to me; does anybody else know if it's true? What happens if you do faint while they're doing it? (Presumably some people do whether they're worried about it beforehand or not?!) Do they have to stop? Will they ban you from giving blood? (There's a lot of stuff on the NBS website about feeling faint, but it all seems to be about feeling faint after giving blood...) (http://www.blood.co.uk/)

janet mcknight

Eat some chocolate or other sweet stuff before you go – that'll keep your blood sugar levels up. Not drinking alcohol the night before might be a good idea too, as that thins the blood and makes clotting harder. Then after you have donated make sure that you take them up on the lie/sit down and the cup of sweet tea and biscuit.

am

One of my friends fainted just before giving blood (yes, she was a bit worried about it) and they sent her away and wouldn't let her give blood again for a year, I think, possibly two or three. But she wasn't banned for life or anything.

sk

My advice: make sure you have a decent meal beforehand, and plenty of fluids to drink; and if you feel ill, don't go. Other than that, there's not much you can do; you'll be lying down while they take the blood and for a while afterwards, so you'd be fairly hard-pushed to faint anyway, to be honest! Let them know you're nervous about it: as a first-timer that's very much to be expected (I've done it four times, and I still get really nervous!), and they'll be very nice to you. I find chatting about something irrelevant helps take my mind off the whole process, and makes me less nervous about it.

sushidog

Your bf is just trying to wind you up. I'm sure if you did actually faint they wouldn't take your blood, but they deal with people who are nervous ALL the time.

The worst part for me is the finger-prick at the start (it HURTS!). That's far worse than the actual donation part.

You'll be lying down all the way through, and you'll be made to stay lying down and resting for ten minutes after the donation is over. You're then encouraged to stay a bit longer for a cuppa and a biscuit, until you're sure you're feeling okay.

You'll be fine. And remember you're doing a Good Thing.

Hmm... is it even possible to faint when you're already lying down??

Just let them know it's your first time and you will be so well looked after.

suzylou

They test for anaemia, and their cut-off is higher than normal. So, if they turn around and say they can't take your blood because your levels aren't high enough that doesn't necessarily mean you're anaemic. They refused me twice, pre-baby, because their cut-off was something like 11 and my blood was 10.9, which isn't anaemic. They turn you away at less than 11 (or whatever) because taking a pint off you then would leave you anaemic, which means they've made you ill.

The blood test they do is a finger-prick, when you're sitting down, so you're unlikely to faint at that (I think). Then they get you to lie down on a couch and that's when they take the blood – if you faint then you are at least lying down, and you won't be the only person who's fainted in that situation. They'll stop taking the blood at that point, but they won't turn you away forever.

If you're going to faint, you're most likely to do so afterwards. Which is why they make you stay on the couch for a bit and then tell you to have a drink and a biscuit before they let you go.

k425

STYES

A stye, according to NHS Direct, is a boil on an eyelash follicle. When I've had styes I've found they just went away eventually after a few days; bathing them in salt water seemed to help speed the process. They're horribly sore though while they last, so much sympathy.

janet mcknight

Once I had a stye. It hurt so much and my eye swelled, so I went to the doctor who gave me two things on prescription: antibiotics, which I ended up having to stop taking, as they gave me thrush, and some eyedrops. The next time I got one, I just left it to go away on its own. It went away after three or four days, and I was whatever two prescriptions are worth (£12 something) better off!

exploitedfairy

Time is generally the best cure. If it hasn't gone in a couple of days or gets huge and out of control, then it's the doctor.

am

Brolene or similar from the chemist can be very effective for this.

clare s

TEACH ME TO BREATHE

Can you teach me to breathe?

Yes, I've read lots of books, but can't seem to get the hang of it. When you're anxious and uptight they always say take a deep breath, but where from – your chest? Stomach? All? Separately? Or together?

My breathing is just a shallow little intake in the top of my chest, hardly noticeable.

aellia

Learn to play a brass instrument. That and singing is pretty much where I learned to breathe, and you do it from your stomach. Try the exercise we used to do in NYCW – breathe all the way out until you have nothing left, then kind of let go of your stomach, let it drop – it breathes all by itself, and doesn't require effort in the same sense that one generally thinks of it.

When I need a *really* deep breath I go stomach first, then top up with top of chest/lungs.

It's not a good idea to lift your shoulders when breathing. Try lying down to breathe – you absolutely cannot lift your shoulders that way! (tip from the book *How Brass Players Do It!*).

bee

Diaphragm. Stomach, basically. The 'breathing all the way out' exercise mentioned above is great. Also, stand with your hands flat on your stomach with the tips of the fingers touching the tips of the fingers on the other hand, then breathe. Your fingers should move apart as you breathe in. Doesn't actually help with the breathing as such though.

mt

Stand and imagine that your whole body – your trunk, from the tops of your legs up to your throat – is an organ pipe. And when you breathe in, the whole cylinder expands widthways, all the way down. When I'm breathing right, my lower back moves outwards, as well as my stomach. (But it took me a couple of years to learn to do it properly.)

westernind

The important word that's nearly always left out is slow. If someone is hyperventilating or otherwise anxious and just told the deep part, there's a good chance they'll take quick deep breaths and be even worse.

Testing on myself now, I automatically breathe deeply when I attempt to breathe slow, but I don't know if it would apply to every one, especially as I have practised deep breathing.

mollydot

If you put your hand flat on your stomach, so that your thumb is along the bottom of your lowest rib, and then breathe in slowly... and keep breathing in...

and breathe in some more... you should feel
your hand being pushed forward. Yoga is quite good
for deep breathing, I think, so that might be worth a
go.

sushidog

You need to locate your diaphragm. It's a flat sheet of
muscle that curves up towards your lungs at rest but
flattens out to increase space when engaged. The best
exercise I was taught to get mine working (I studied
the flute to near-pro level) was to stand with feet
shoulders-width apart and bend over at the waist,
letting the upper body relax. Once you're nice and
loose through your back and shoulders, start barking
like a dog. The muscle you can feel moving just above
your stomach with every woof is your diaphragm.
The second stage of the exercise is to slowly straighten
up again, barking all the way, without losing the
movement in the diaphragm when you woof. Once
you've cracked that, concentrate on making that
muscle move when you breathe in, let your back
expand as well as your front, and you should be
breathing properly.

cazmanian minx

If you lie on your back with a piece of white paper on
your stomach you'll be able to see quite clearly
whether you're breathing all the way down. It's not
something most people do.

ailbhe

SLEEP ISSUES

Have any of you ladies tried a natural sleep aid like melatonin? Cheers for any advice/thoughts.

mtb0001

I've used melatonin and found it to be very good. No heavy head feeling in the morning. Sominex do a one-a-night thing too which is also very good. Nytol just did nothing at all for me.

cookwitch

Another thumbs-up for melatonin; I use it occasionally, when I'm having trouble sleeping due to disturbed sleep patterns or stress, and I've found it gets me to sleep without any negative effects. Other sleep-aids (Nytol, prescription drugs) tend to give me a horrible hangover, or just don't do anything much.

sushidog

I tried melatonin, having always had problems sleeping – and it didn't work for me... I guess it depends why you need to sleep (i.e. just been away, and jetlag) or just not being able to sleep... but one thing that worked for me, was magnesium – one of those things my mum told me, that apparently if you take it it helps you sleep. I have no idea why. Nowadays I avoid caffeine after 4 pm, try not to use the computer for an hour before I go to bed, and have a herbal tea of some kind (usually with camomile in it). If I'm not too sneezy and haven't taken any antihistamines through the day, a Piriton sometimes helps too.

sw

CYSTITIS RELIEF

Lemon barley water! People recommended this to me for the same reason a few weeks back, and it was surprisingly effective. Also wearing cotton/natural fibre knickers.

sarah malaise

Lots of water, as well as cranberry juice. Wear cotton pants, and don't wear very tight trousers! Also, don't wear pants to bed if you usually do. Cranberry supplements (available from a health store) will probably work out cheaper than lots of cranberry juice.

*_mardybum_*

If things don't improve and you DO go to the GP, please make sure he doesn't give you trimethoprim as it has a 33% failure rate (due to resistance and other mechanisms). Something like cefalexin (95% success rate) would be better.

genie22

Bicarbonate of soda, dissolved in water; that's basically what the expensive sachets you buy at the chemist contain, but you can buy a tub of bicarb far cheaper and use it for cooking as well! Just dissolve a teaspoonful in half a pint of water and drink at least once every hour (if you can manage it, drink a glass of cranberry juice every hour as well). You will spend the day running to the loo, but it should help.

sushidog

During a recent and particularly bad bout of cystitis, I asked a pharmacist whether there was anything available on the market that wasn't a nasty, synthetic cranberry flavour. She came up trumps with an over-the-counter remedy named Effercitrate. For relief, you dissolve two tablets in a tumbler of water and drink it as you would any other remedy. It tastes vaguely of lemon, is reasonably palatable, and far more pleasant than the revolting cranberry sachets. Most importantly, I felt relief within an hour! I didn't quite believe that this could be true, so decided to try it again before alerting everyone to the wonders. It turns out that it really *is* that effective. Once again, the relief was rapid.

Effercitrate. Remember the name. You'll never go back to drinking pure cranberry, or dissolving sachets of nastiness ever again!

pipistrellus

Lemon barley water and a hot water bottle – works every time for me!!

desiring cairo

EAR
SYRINGING

Has anyone ever had their ears syringed? I'm getting a little concerned on the hearing front. My boyfriend mumbles a fair bit and I have a lot of trouble hearing him. It's easier with other people, but today I realised that my ears feel 'blocked'. Like you get when flying. If I yawn they kind of pop a little bit then settle back down again. It seems to be low-register sound that I have trouble with, as I can hear the TV and music just fine. I get woken up by the 'click' of the CD just before my alarm goes off too, so I'm fairly sure that my actual hearing level is okay, which lead me to wonder if my ears needed syringing.

cookwitch

Ages back, yes. I was told to put some sort of oil (from the pharmacy) in for a few days beforehand, then syringed. I would rate it as unpleasant rather than painful and a very odd feeling. I suspect I need it done again due to wax build-up.

blue_cat

I had my ears syringed last year, when a bad cold caused wax build-up which impaired my hearing and felt *horrible*. I used ear drops for a week or so beforehand, which helped a bit but not much. The syringing was a little uncomfortable but not painful. It can make you feel slightly dizzy, but that doesn't last long, and it does get rid of wax. The nurse who did mine did warn me that in some cases regular ear syringing actually seems to increase the production of wax, so it's a last resort.

sushidog

I've had it done a couple of times. Earwax can build up and harden if you spend a lot of time with your head under water. Long baths are my problem, but swimming can do it as well.

I was also advised to put oil in them every morning and night for a week before the syringing, but my doctor said there wasn't anything special about the oil and normal cooking oil would be fine. I bought a little bottle with a dropper attached to the lid, put in some sunflower oil and did what she said. Now I use some of it whenever I feel my ears might be getting clogged again, and haven't had to be syringed again since.

secretrebel

I went deaf in one ear through wax build-up when I was 16 and the GP syringed it out. It hurt like hell and a solid plug came out. Ever since I've managed with warm oil (warm a teaspoon in hot water, then warm the oil on the spoon – you don't want it *actually* warm) and letting it drain out overnight.

ailbhe

DECON-
GESTING

I'm currently full of a cold. The cold (and cough) I can deal with, but now my ears are all bunged. I can barely hear anything and they're quite painful. Does anyone have any advice on how to unblock them?

princesswannabe

It's your sinuses so you'll need a decongestant. Try holding your head over a basin of hot water with a towel over your head (so the steam goes in your face).Various Beechams' hot lemon/Strepsils-type things might help as well. Also, over the counter-wise you can try Sudafed. The problem with drug-type decongestants is that if you use them too much, once you stop it all comes back with a vengeance.

sara

Sudafed – or another cold cure with a drug that will unblock your nose.

gg

You may have heavy wax build-up, in which case ear drops such as Otex should help. If they don't clear the problem up within five days or so, you could get your ears syringed to remove the wax; you'll need to make an appointment with your local nurse to do this, and you'll need to let them know you've been using drops for a few days, otherwise they won't do it.

sushidog

I'd second the suggestion of steam inhalation as it's good for clearing the tubes that run between your ears and throat, so should help relieve the pressure in your ears. Plus it's good for your pores too. I find putting a bit of menthol and eucalyptus in the water helps, although if you do, try not to breathe in through your mouth as it can taste a bit weird.

aligoestonz

IRON DEFICIENCY

My blood tests say I have an iron deficiency. I have 14.5 thingies of ferritin, whereas (from craning my neck over and looking at the computer screen on the practice nurse's desk) apparently I should have between 20 and 500. Nice nurse says this should explain why I'm feeling abnormally tired, and the minor hair loss, which is what sent me to the doctor in the first place. Also, from reading the NHS Direct info on anaemia, it might account for a couple of recent unexplained headaches. I never normally get headaches.

What I'm wondering is, what could the root cause be? I'm 41, I don't have particularly heavy periods, but I do eat a fairly healthy diet although not much red meat. The iron tablets I've been asked to take address the symptoms, but I'd like to know what else I need to change. And the leaflet says, not to take them within two hours of a list of foods, including tea, coffee, dairy products, wholegrain bread/cereals, eggs, or the tablets might not work properly. What's that about then?

westernind

I'd only ever heard of not taking them with tea because it stops them absorbing properly. I'd assume it must be the same with the other foods.

You need to make sure you're eating lots of green leafy vegetables I think.

This may be helpful, sorry not got long online so I just Googled it and this one looked good! http://www.healthcastle.com/iron.shtml.

rebecca mcallister

One of the B vitamins is related to anaemia – you can be eating all the iron-rich foods you like but if you're lacking the relevant B vit it won't help. It's B12 I think.

caroline

EPO

This is a public service announcement on behalf of the PMS, SAD and Generally Grumpy/Upset party. Try evening primrose oil. I have crawled in here mewling and gnawing about being alternately miserable and angry, sometimes PMS, sometimes just because I Am Me. EPO is wonderful. It restores perspective, easing the excessive tension of whatever emotion is flooding clarity, and makes Life and the problems, difficulties, banalities and generalities so much more straight-forward to manage – mainly because there is less excessive You to manage! And without feeling drugged – which is important to me. I have been using it for over a month and the change has been amazing. Quite simply amazing.

kimkali

Don't use if trying to get pregnant... actually, you can use it up until ovulation, but it shouldn't be used after that.

ladyynara

Starflower oil can suit people who don't get on with/ notice the effects of EPO – it's a more concentrated version. Also, two of the EPO gelatine capsules or ½ tsp of the oil mixed into your fave moisturiser/body lotion makes it wonderfully rich.

laumiere

COELIAC DISEASE

I have been diagnosed with coeliac disease and I need to start a gluten-free diet. So now I need your help. I'm pretty sure some of you are eating gluten-free for whatever reason. So, what's good? What should I watch out for – hidden gluten? What pasta is really disgusting? What cookery books are good? Where can I get calcium from if I'm supposed to double my daily intake?

I'm asymptomatic (tested because my Mum's coeliac was diagnosed after she had neurological problems) so I'm not likely to start feeling better, but I'm going to do this so that I don't have the same problems she has in 20 years' time. Remind me of this when I crave a beer or, worse, a Jaffa cake...

k425

Things to watch out for mainly include fillers in stuff, from what I can tell. So rusky stuff in sausages and burgers (my bro's main diet!) is a problem, and my mam has to make sure she gets 100% meat everything. Going to a proper butcher's is good for that, though Co-op sausages are gluten-free. Come to think of it, I think Co-op are generally pretty good for noting these things on the packaging. They also do a gluten-free beer, called Discovery, which is a bit dearer for less beer than normal, but still.

Tamari is a gluten-free alternative to soy sauce, which I quite like. Flavoured crisps generally have gluten in the MSG.

bee

Watch out for Chinese food, which contains high levels of monosodium glutamate. So you can't have that, I'm afraid. Most flavoured crisps also use MSG, but Potato Heads don't (all flavours), Kettle Chips don't, and ready salted ones don't.

I've found that Asda, although it has a tiny weeny free-from section, actually changes products regularly, so there seems to always be something new in.

www.goodnessdirect.co.uk is a great site, as you can pick gluten-free from the list of special diets, and it lists everything it sells that is gluten-free. Bit pricey with it, I imagine (not bought anything from there yet as I'm waiting for my cupboards/freezer to empty!).

*_mardybum_*

BINGO WINGS

Right, I've got a pair of hand-weights. What do I do with them to get rid of my fat upper arms? I think I have to lift the weights such that the arms

**straighten with the lift, for example lifting up-
wards from behind the neck. But should my
elbows be pointing forward or to the sides? And
holding the weights with knuckles forward,
backward or to the sides? Help!**

pp

To get rid of the fat on your arms, you need to do
cardiovascular exercise, rather than resistance training.
Using weights will improve your muscle tone, but
won't get rid of fat.

Some exercises that would help tone that area are:

Hold the weights down by your sides, palms facing
forwards. Slowly and smoothly bend your elbows to
bring the weights up to your shoulders, and then
slowly and smoothly return them to your sides.
Repeat. Make sure you don't jerk them up or down,
the movement has to be slow and steady, and you
should be able to feel a slight ache after a few reps,
which will let you know exactly which muscles are
working! Try not to lock your elbows when you
straighten your arms.

Second, hold the weights beside your ears, palms
towards your head. Slowly and steadily, lift them to
arm's length with your arms straight up. Slowly and
steadily lower again, bending your elbow. Repeat.
Again, don't lock your elbows.

Third, hold the weights at arm's length by your
sides, palms facing your thighs. Slowly and smoothly
raise your arms sideways, without bending them, to
shoulder height, and then slowly and smoothly lower
them again.

To lose the fat as well, do some cardiovascular stuff:
brisk walking, jogging, skipping, dancing, vigorous

sex, vigorous housework, aerobics, swimming, cycl-
ing, rowing... anything that increases your pulse rate
and leaves you a bit breathless. Ideally, do half an hour
to 40 minutes a day.

sushidog

OMEGA 3

**I understand that eating oily fish helps brain
function and memory, but as I'm vegetarian this
isn't much use to me. Are there any vegetarian equivalents of whatever the good stuff in
them is, and are there any other foods that boost
intelligence?**

suicideally

Boots flax oil capsules – it's omega 3 you're looking
for and this is also found in flax.

cc

I believe it's omega 3 and omega 6 fatty acids. http://
www.vegsoc.org/info/omega3.html – info here on
omega 3; seems omega 6 isn't such an issue.

jk

I think the key ingredient (as it were) is omega oils –
omega 3 and omega 6. I know they're now putting

these into products like yoghurt drinks (specifically, the Vitality ones), but they're also found in nuts and seeds. Vitamins generally are good for the brain, so make sure you're getting as varied and healthy a diet as possible; B vitamins (found in marmite, beans, and some dairy) are especially good. Keeping your blood sugar steady should also help, so go for low-GI foods, which give you a steady release of energy, rather than sugary stuff which gives you spikes and troughs.

Rosemary and sage are both supposed to boost the memory and the brain generally, so it's worth using them lots! In fact, a study a couple of years ago found that chewing a couple of sage leaves every day seems to stave off dementia in the elderly, as well as cleaning the teeth and giving you fresh breath!

sushidog

Steady with the sage, it's strong stuff: some of my herb books warn against overuse. Best to check before daily use – it can have some hormonal effects, and sage oil should never be used during pregnancy or if you are prone to epilepsy.

I've not yet spotted any warnings with rosemary, but as it's so strongly flavoured you'd probably have to eat an unfeasible amount before it harmed you.

md

Having done some work on this and been to a conference about omega 3 I think I can help.

Flax, linseed and microalgae are also rich in omega 3 – fish get their omega 3 by eating the algae. The only problem with some vegetarian sources is that there are different types of omega 3, and to get the same thing you would get from fish oils you need about ten times the amount of a vegetable source – and they give a different type of omega 3 (ALA and not DHA or EPA, which are the ones that help the brain and stuff – DHA mostly) – this refers mostly to flax and linseed, as microalgae are rarer in the market and harder to find in regular products in the supermarket.

tt

QUITTING SMOKING

Ask everyone you ever share cigarettes with to not share theirs with you if/when you ask/beg. If you can, avoid seeing people you usually smoke with in the context where you normally smoke with them for a few weeks (e.g. if you always meet up with smoker friends in a pub, avoid the pub – try and do different things until you're over the worst). If you slip up, don't say 'Oh sod it then' and go back to it: quit again.

jinn

If you're in a pub, try to cut down on the amount of alcoholic drinks you have. When I was giving up I found that the more drunk I was, the harder it was to remember WHY I wasn't smoking. Also, try drinking something you wouldn't normally – hopefully you won't then associate it with smoking at the same time.

And buy some crisps to keep your hands/mouth occupied when you're craving a fag. Hope this is of some help – it worked for me!

misswilde

Take up knitting! Gives you something to do with your hands, which is the thing that always gets me, because if I'm in a pub and I'm not smoking I'll be tearing up the beer mats, rolling a bit of paper that I found in my pocket into a tiny ball, picking at my nails, whatever. I am one of Life's Fiddlers.

I only really social smoke, and I often go months at a time without smoking, so giving up for me has never really been a big deal. But if I'm going out to the pub and I don't want to end up smoking, I take knitting with me. As long as you can cope with the mockery, it's great.

la bias

Don't ever tell yourself that Just One Won't Matter. It will: even if you stick at one, you may well start the whole craving thing again. Steer clear of smoky places if you're feeling a bit of a craving – they'll make it worse.

If you can do without nicotine gum etc., do – it helps a lot in not having a cigarette, but it doesn't stop your body thinking that nicotine is fun.

Niacin – vitamin B3 – helped take the edge off my cravings. If the cravings do get really bad, and you get mood swings and headaches, drink lots of water and fruit juice, and suck niacin tablets.

Very best of luck: it's hard, but it's worth it.

tamaranth

TOOTHACHE

Clove oil on cotton wool directly on the tooth (but it's incredibly strong and can be very unpleasant).

Swill tepid salt water round the tooth.

My mum swears by this one: apply Sensodyne toothpaste (other sensitive toothpastes probably work too) directly on to the tooth causing the pain.

Go to the dentist asap! If you're afraid, find a surgery that specialises in anxious patients. If I can get around my dentist fears, anyone can!

fa

My husband swears by clove oil as well; actually the chemists sell it, and applying it with a cotton bud (new one every time, natch) can be better than anything else; however, a clean finger does in an emergency. Long-term use can cause ulceration though.

wyvernfriend

DEALING WITH PANIC ATTACKS

I started having them a couple of months ago, and what makes them different from other sorts of anxiety/panic I've had in the past is their totally random and unexplained nature. Which makes them very frightening and difficult to control.

What helps? Well, I'm still in the early stages of finding out, but since I started taking a few particular steps I haven't had any more full-blown attacks.

First, I did have a think about what was bringing them on. There were common themes in the situations when they arose, and just knowing what they are is helpful. Can you think of anything that makes an attack more likely?

Second, I got myself seen by a health professional. This helped most of all, as until I did I was convinced I was actually dying of something physical every time one came on. In a way I was 'lucky' in that I had a massively bad one in a club. My friends were able to get me to a paramedic, who diagnosed panic attack very quickly.

Third, I've taken up activities that make me more aware of my passing mental states and so I feel more in control of them. For me, this is meditation and a lot of soul-searching, but there are all sorts of other ways.

I've also read up on the subject and found some helpful tips on what you can do physically when you feel one coming on.

But yes, I know how scary they are, and despite all this I am still prone to them and very wary about a lot of activities I used to enjoy as a result.

starmix

To combat them, I used a combination of breathing exercises, beta-blockers (for a few months so that I could get them under control), high-dosage vitamin B, and some other relaxation techniques before bed-time. I also had some energy healing which I think helped, but I know some people think it's hokey. I also changed my diet, cutting out caffeine and most sugar. But it's been about four years since I had a full-scale panic attack, so something must have worked!

Please don't be worried about speaking to your GP about it, because they will be able to offer advice on anything newer that might help.

lm

I found that knowing what they were was the first step to helping get them under control. Breathing exercises, other relaxation exercises, decaf coffee all worked for me. My GP referred me to a counsellor to help with depression and stress, which also helped.

kate atkin-wright

I have an acute anxiety disorder which I've had since I was a child. Counselling didn't help much, because in my case the problem is chemical not emotional. I went on a variety of antidepressants, which stopped the anxiety but caused so many other problems I stopped them. But there are things you can do, such as:

- Rationalising it: remember anxiety/panic is caused by fear of the future, i.e. what if x happens, what if I never x, what if this never goes etc. Try to ground yourself in the present.
- Paper bags. Rebreathe into a paper bag; it helps to restore your air levels to what they should be (i.e. you can get too much oxygen through hyperventilation).
- Exercise lots. Exercising helps to keep your serotonin levels healthy and it releases endorphins to give you a good happy boost. I swear by this.
- Eat as healthily as you can, plenty of fresh fruit and veg.
- Ensure you get enough sleep. The minute I lack sleep my mind starts to go nuts.
- You might not need this as you may not suffer from this, but I get SAD, which can trigger panic attacks. A SAD lamp helps loads.

siren

COGNITIVE THERAPY

Has anyone here ever tried cognitive therapy? What were your experiences of it? Did you do it

**privately or on the NHS? If you could go back
would you do it again?**

hazyjayne

I had cognitive therapy to get me driving again after a
car accident. It was very good. I'm not sure to this day
how or why it all worked, but it took me about seven
sessions I think. I did it privately (£50/session) and
was compensated by the accident insurance.

land_girl

CBT helped somewhat with my depression, but was
most successful in helping with my anxiety problem –
it uses fairly simple techniques to help you understand
your thought processes, and helps you to find the
'break' or 'screw up' in the chain that you need to fix
in order to feel better. I had it on the NHS after being
referred through my doctor.

If I felt like I was losing my grip again I might go
back for one or two sessions to help me remember
how to handle my thought processes, but generally I
feel that, once you've done it and learnt it, it's probably with you for life.

halluciphy

Yes, 15 years ago, on the NHS, referred by my then
GP. Was in a pretty bad way at the time. Concentrated on addressing the 'automatic thinking' that
if I didn't do everything perfectly I'd failed, and gave
me a set of tools for making complex decisions.
(One of the decisions subsequently made was 'jack in
my overly high-powered yuppie accountancy job

and lifestyle and go do a degree in philosophy'; this was a good decision, but seemed very hard at the time.)

It got me functioning, it was a good thing. Didn't fix my long-term issues, but then I don't think it was designed to do that. With hindsight, yes, I'd do it again.

westernind

Yes, I had CBT about three years ago, on the NHS, via a referral from occupational health at work. I found it incredibly useful to be able to identify patterns in my behaviour and reactions to stress, although I found some of the exercises pretty hard at the time. On the whole, though, it made it possible for me to get on with my life.

I would also recommend a book called *Overcoming Childhood Trauma Using CBT* (although I appreciate it may not be relevant in your case).

dw

Yes, I've tried it. I was lucky, as I had private medical insurance and an employer willing to push for the very best treatment for me.

I did benefit from CBT in some ways, but it wasn't as helpful as it could have been because I'd been wrongly diagnosed with depression. I was actually suffering from chronic fatigue syndrome, and was barely depressed at all. However, I did enough to prove to myself that you CAN change the way you think if you try hard enough, and you want to. It's a very interactive process, and it makes you feel as if you're doing something to help yourself – an idea that was really important to me. So I'd recommend giving it a go if it's offered to you.

If you're having trouble getting CBT on the NHS, and you can't go private, you can help yourself by getting hold of a copy of *Mind Over Mood* and working through the exercises. Obviously it's better if you have someone to talk to and guide you through it, but I reckon you could do some of it yourself.

kate b

CBT – it's great. It's the only thing that's ever really helped with my depression and chronic fatigue. I'm currently on my second batch. It does, however, require work on your part, and if you're not prepared to put that in and trust to a certain extent that the therapist knows what they're doing, you're unlikely to get much from it. I think that the advantage it has over analysis or other psychotherapy is that it doesn't attempt to engage with what's on the emotional level, where the battle can be too much, but instead on a practical level, dealing with where you are now and what you can do about it.

sesquipedality

I had it (privately) for a while when I was at college. I found it great in the long term (in that some of the techniques and tools I learned from it I still use, and it helped cure (or at least alleviate) a long depression and other destructive problems), but at the time I found it difficult – the results (for me) were slow in coming, and so for a while I was convinced it wasn't working at all. I would recommend it, but also suggest keeping up 'normal' counselling too (I had counselling through the university, but stopped when I started therapy – I think I should have kept at both of them).

jinn

CALMING/
CAN'T STOP
CRYING –
ADVICE?

Does anyone here know any way to stop myself crying/hyperventilating and make myself get down to bloody work?

bee

You got any Bach rescue remedy there m'dear? That's pretty good; also Kalms. Or, my usual trick, have a bloody good, absolutely hysterical cry and let it all go until you're worn out and then start work again.

I wonder if dark chocolate would help? I know it's good for depression. Camomile tea is supposed to be good for calming people down too.

cookwitch

Argent nits is good, it's a homeopathic thing, you can get it in Boots.

tooth_fairy

St John's Wort can be helpful in some cases. Exercise may help, particularly something like yoga or tai chi, which helps calm and focus the mind as well as providing physical exercise. Breathing exercises can also be good; if you're hyperventilating, try breathing in to a slow count of four and then out to a slow count of five for a few minutes.

sushidog

If you can take a few minutes for yourself, breathing exercises along with some basic 'reprogramming' stuff may be helpful; I know the 'go to your happy place' stuff sounds like awful rubbish, but it can be useful. Also, if you find yourself drifting off-focus from work and dwelling on a bad situation, giving yourself a mental shake and deliberately changing the subject (of your internal monologue) can be quite effective. You may need to give yourself some time later, when you're not at work, to cry/dwell on stuff/work it through/whatever, as just repressing it could be a bad plan in the long term!

sushidog

Go for a quick walk (five mins), then set a timer and work for 15 minutes. Or work out what the very next step is. Then do that.

mollydot

Rosemary essential oil is good for concentration, and if you are thesis writing and deep in the panic stage I recommend getting up, going downstairs, making yourself a cup of something hot, and while the kettle's boiling, having a good dance in the kitchen – turn the radio on, and just dance to whatever's playing. I used to have to do this to keep myself on track, and figured that about four minutes' mad dancing ever hour or so was a really healthy thing, and it cleared my head.

nb

I had a phase when I couldn't stop crying a couple of years ago. I'm trying to think how it got better, or why it got better, and not coming up with anything that has a definite cause and effect. But, um, some of the things I did around the time it started getting better: Demanded more space for myself, instead of always trying to please other people. Tried to get more sleep. Decided to quit the job that was eating my self-esteem. Broke up with the person who criticised me 24 hours a day.

I thought at the time that I was being totally irrational and crying over nothing, but I'd just lost sight of the things that were actually upsetting me and had come to think of them as perfectly normal. Probably all totally irrelevant. But maybe my only valid point is that it does get better, it does pass, it won't stay that way forever.

bluedevi

I think also you need to remember that crying is not wrong. I'm not usually a person that cries, and I've realised recently that the occasional tearfulness I get (the kind where I do that hand-wavy 'ooh, I'm sorry, I'm fine, oh god' thing, when I'm trying to have a conversation with someone at work, or when I find tears running down my cheeks when I'm on the bus) – that's emotion that needs to come out. It's

expression. Sometimes it's embarrassing, but it's feelings making themselves known, because maybe they
don't have room to be expressed in other ways

tb

Not only is crying not wrong, and a good way of
releasing stress and tension, but it's actually proactive
and releases happy endorphins into your brain. Hence
feeling better after a good cry. I find when I go
through a happy period where I haven't cried for ages,
I really really need to watch a sad film – like I need to
get my endorphin high that's been missing through
life actually being good to me for a bit.

silke

ANGER MANAGEMENT

**Does anyone have tips on anger management? I
have a violent side that only appears once a year or
so, in an emotional ketchup blast kind of way, but
I don't want to have that violent side at all. I have
trouble controlling my emotional reactions to
situations and I really need to learn how not to
react inappropriately. Sure, it wouldn't be good to
be an emotionless robot, but having control over
the displaying of emotions would be a good thing.**

**In books, it suggests things like hitting phone-
books with hoses, taking up some kind of sport**

such as a martial art, writing angry things in a diary, writing letters to those you are angry with and burning them, screaming in your car with the windows up, etc. Books also seem to suggest calming activities such as relaxing baths, etc.

British Association of Anger Management has a list of helpful things. It suggests counting backwards from 20, which I suppose might give me time to actually act in a more rational and reasonable kind of way as opposed to a crazy, psychotic emotional way.

judith_crunch

A year of therapy (not just for the anger) has helped me control my feelings a bit more. I've also been known to lock myself in the bathroom at work and kick the walls.

Writing letters and burning/tearing them up have helped me in the short term, but I always feel like the anger hasn't entirely dissipated. I find that having a friend I know I can call up and rant at, without being told how to fix the problem in return, really helps. I call my best mate and she just sympathises with me. It makes me feel better to have someone agreeing with me that X is a wanker and must die (for example).

lozette

Anything that gets you out of the situation, even temporarily, is good, if you're prone to flare up. So counting backwards from 20, or taking ten deep, slow breaths (doubly helpful because it helps to slow your heartbeat and suppress the adrenaline rush!), going and getting a glass of water, going for a quick walk etc., can all help in the immediate situation.

In the medium term, sometimes talking through what has made you angry with someone, either the person involved or an unbiased friend, can be helpful, as can martial arts or exercises such as yoga or t'ai chi. In fact, exercise in general is good for reducing stress, so that might be helpful. I've used the 'writing a letter and burning it/throwing it away' thing, but that's more for the sort of 'slow' grudge-bearing anger which eats away at you for weeks, than the 'ketchup blast' (good term, by the way!) that you describe.

In the long term it might be worth having a look at the situations in which you've exploded, and trying to figure out what set you off; it may be that the 'triggers' are linked to an unresolved issue which could be dealt with in some way, and that might then make you less likely to lose control in future, or it may give you a way of avoiding likely triggers.

sushidog

Once a year is such a rare event it sounds like it could be difficult to tackle in the usual way. It would be simpler if you were angry say, at times of the month, or regularly. Once yearly is going to catch you out.

Perhaps you need to sit down and write up an account of each episode you have experienced. First try and describe it to yourself in detail – the build up, the people, the event, the aftermath. Then read through each episode and try and see what links them – a common thread, a particular rare situation you find yourself in, blah blah. It may not be so much an exercise in managing anger, more an unlocking of self-knowledge. If you can study yourself in these situations, perhaps find knowledge of a link or trigger with them, you'll be better prepared to recognise the next potential scenario and thus side-step it.

md

COPING WITH NIGHT-TIME ANXIETY

Personally I find that putting on the light, even only briefly, reassures you that the room is normal. Try listening to some music, or I have a handy little machine that makes wave noises that calms and sends me to sleep.

zoefruitcake

If there's no cause, I get up and read or make a drink and sit in the living room for a bit.

k425

I always used to read a book. An old favourite rather than the latest thriller, or I'd be awake for hours. Now I share my bed and can't put the light on, I play Scrabble on my GameBoy Advance. That back-lit screen has been my life-saver. I find I often wake up in the morning with it still clutched in my hand.

kate atkin-wright

Camomile tea, or valerian (or a valerian-containing pill like Quiet Life) can help.

lozette

Here's an exercise I use: Sit up. Close your eyes. Breathe normally. Count your breaths. Start again at one every time you get to ten. Don't think about anything else – just focus on your breathing. If you find your mind wandering, that's OK, just start counting again at one. It makes your mind blank and it's wonderfully calming, for me anyway. I can feel my system relaxing and slowing down when I do it.

Other than that, the usual stuff – no caffeine after 6 pm, don't eat for a couple of hours before you go to bed, no booze, make sure your room is comfortable and at a good temperature, etc. etc.

cartographer

Everything you need to know about coping with it: http://www.anxietyandstress.com/sys-tmpl/dealing-withpanic/.

siren

Visualisation: takes a bit of prep though. Have a think (before you have an anxious attack, possibly during the day) of a place you can visualise in your mind, a place that soothes and relaxes you. It might be a made-up place, or a childhood holiday memory (walking on the beach, wiggling toes in the sand, stretching out for a snooze in the sun). Practise the visualisation a little bit until you have the scenario neatly worked out in your head.

Later, when you get a night-time attack, retrieve your pre-prepared soothing scenario, play it out in your head, focus on it until you relax (and hopefully nod off again). I find this works better than getting up or putting the light on (which kind of ruins the, 'I have a busy day tomorrow and I really need to sleep, not twat about in the middle of the night' mindset). Doesn't work for everyone though – some people aren't keen on painting pictures in their heads.

md

I listen to the BBC World Service on the radio. I turn it down low so I can only just hear it, and I fall asleep quickly every time, but if I do happen to wake up again I tend to learn all sorts of interesting things and therefore don't have to think about what's worrying me.

mendi

Second the camomile tea or herbal pills – try Quiet Night, available from Boots.

I get this, too – not exactly anxiety, but brain in overdrive. I have learnt to get up and leave the bed when it happens. It has happened less since I've been exercising more.

juggzy

Get up, go write a list of whatever's bugging you, go read a book on the loo for half an hour, decide that it's cold and silly o'clock and bed would be a good plan.

OK, so this possibly only works when the anxiety is caused by thinking too much about work and ending up with to-do lists circling round in your head that you get irrationally worried you'll forget by the morning – but getting sufficiently chilly that bed seems cunning does work (though may get you grumbled at by other resident(s) of the bed.

CDs on quietly in the background can help with getting back to sleep. Tapes are bad because they click noisily when they run to the end.

sea_of_flame

BACH RESCUE REMEDY

When I was in the town this morning I picked up some of that Bach rescue remedy spray that I keep hearing people on here say is great. I had a quick go of it then and there, but is it supposed to taste so vile?! I know it says it's a grape alcohol solution, but to me it just tastes like pure alcohol or a very cheap vodka! Does that sound about right? Also, if you were feeling stressed or anxious, how long should it take to work if it was going to?

rebecca mcallister

Yeah, it does taste vile, don't worry about it. You could try putting a few drops in a glass of water and swallowing it that way, though it doesn't work as quickly if you do that.

Typically it calms me down a bit about 10–15 minutes after taking it – usually I take quite a bit though.

vgl

Yeah, it tastes like vodka. If you down the whole bottle in one go it gets you drunk too (this is what usually happens with me on a plane journey – drink entire bottle of Bachs stuff, relax a bit, continue drinking, end up with stinking hangover mid flight, feel sick for the rest of the way. But at least I'm not running up and down the aisles screaming OH MY GOD WE'RE ALL GOING TO DIE!!!!!!!!!!).

sara

I used to put a few drops into my bottle of water at work, which I actually really liked after I got used to the taste.

seren

Miscellaneous

MUSIC PROGRAM

Gadget thing I've just discovered and now can't live without is www.musicbrainz.org. You download a program and it tags and sorts your music automatically. Which when you've got as many songs as I do is a godsend.

es

WINDY BABY

Anyone out there have any REAL advice on how to help a month-old, very painful, windy baby? He's mostly fine when he's sitting up, but as soon as we lie him down he starts to howl. Or, he'll make VERY loud grunting noises, and whimpers, while drawing his knees up to his chest.

This will go on from when you put him down until you get him up for his next feed. Not good when mummy is trying to sleep, and certainly not good for baby.

We've been using the Dr Brown's (BabyBFree) bottles the last couple of days – we give him a dose of Infacol before each feed, AND he's been

prescribed Gaviscon for acid reflux. Unfortunately the label on his new formula (Neocate,
which is prescribed as he is allergic to the proteins in milk) says that it may cause more wind,
so we're fighting uphill on this one.

Anyone? Any tried and tested methods? Even
good advice for how to bring up the wind that he
has?

mn

A position that seems to work for some babies: lie him
face-down along your (non-dominant) arm, so that
your hand is under his nappy and his head is next to
your elbow, with his body supported by your arm. In
this position, you should be able to swing or rock him
gently, and use your spare hand to rub or pat his back.

sushidog

Massage his tummy in a circular motion (around the
belly button). That's the advice I was given when I
had IBS – based on the best way to help colicky
babies. Press with the heel of your hand (not too hard,
but enough to relieve the pressure of the wind).

elethe

If he's got colic, there isn't anything you can do. This
is bad, because it means everything you try will only
relieve it slightly. This is good, though, because when
he's crying you'll know that it's not your fault. You're
not doing anything wrong.

My eldest had colic, and it was just a matter of
finding the most comfortable positions for him,

movements, bottles etc. The best bottles I found were the Avent disposable ones, which they don't make any more, because the bag collapsed as he fed, so no air could come in.

From around three months old you're allowed to give paracetamol liquid, but colic stops at three months anyway.

His preferred sleeping position was on his tummy, knees drawn up, on my chest, with me stroking his back. In the daytime he had to be carried around in a sling. Find out what works for you.

I never found any improvement with using Infacol, and wasn't very happy about giving so much silicon to a newborn baby.

Also, take a break. Hand him over to granny or a friend for half an hour or so and have a good sleep.

Keep talking to your health visitor, and if it's not starting to pass as he approaches three months, that's when you need to worry.

If your breasts are still leaking any milk, try and pump or squeeze off a few drops, and (checking with the health visitor whether he's allergic to your milk first) add a tiny amount to his bottles – it might help him to digest them.

vf

Babies are very very seldom allergic to their mother's milk. It's a very rare condition and he would be in hospital by now if he had it. It's entirely possible for them to react to, for example, cow's milk proteins in their mother's milk but this is extremely easy to fix: Mum just cuts out dairy products completely.

mjf

I don't know whether you're breastfeeding – if so, drink fennel tea yourself and that may help the baby. If not, make some fennel tea and give a small amount to him – not too much, as you don't want to fill him up on nutrition-free liquids.

One of my friends made an artificial shoulder – cushions on the top of the settee – and would lie his daughter over that and pat and rub her back while he did other things. She would often go to sleep like that.

If it's when you lie him down, try putting him in a sling or baby carrier so he's still upright – being close to you he may well burp quickly, but even if he doesn't he's likely to go to sleep. And if he's attached to you, you can lean back in a comfy chair on your bed and nap too, without worrying that you'll drop him. Or stick him in a bouncy chair – fairly upright, the bouncing can help bring the wind up, and you can bounce the chair with a foot while leaning back with your eyes closed. Oh. OldBloke used to have some success putting YoungBloke over his shoulder and walking up and down the stairs. The extra bumping seemed to help soothe him even if he didn't burp.

My son was a complete bugger to burp. He just didn't. Even with Infacol. At best he'd bring up the wind and then bloomin' swallow it again. So we'd hear it grumbling through his system until he'd draw his legs up to his chest and rattle his nappies with farts that sounded painful. So I really do sympathise with you.

In your darkest moments, repeat to yourself the Mother's Mantra: This too shall pass.

k425

The homeopathic remedy nux vomica is good for trapped wind, sore tummies etc. if you are that way inclined. We used it on my son (and still do) and it works really well.

sa

There is a baby massage movement, I can't remember the name of it but it involves resting your baby stomach-down on your arms, their head is facing down and there is the weight of your arms on their stomach. I found this very helpful with my baby and they really like it.

tooth fairy

FOOD FOR CHILDREN

My little girl is going through that phase of not wanting to eat anything unusual or different from her usual foods.

First, I was wondering if anyone has good methods for handling this, tempting toddlers to eat the unknown (she's 3)? Second, for the ladies who have children, what is their favourite food, do you have a recipe for a great kids meal that you could share?

For the ladies who don't have children, do you have a favourite childhood meal and can I have the recipe? Another weekend of fishfingers and

Weetabix and I am going to pull my hair out in frustration!

tooth_fairy

I've been using those vitamin gummy bear things from Boots; giving vitamins does at least relieve some of the anxiety of them not getting the nutrients.

tooth_fairy

Going on my own childhood...

- Disguise things – but not like mashing sprouts in with potatoes (shudder!).
- I used to like bananas if they were sliced with the skins on. You can then unwrap each slice like a banana 'sweetie'.
- Apples – cut them into chips.
- Carrots – cut into goldfish shapes.
- You can try involving her more with cooking or baking – she may be more likely to eat something if she's helped to make it. This is a messy solution but I used to have fun helping bake scones with my nanna from an early age. Things like pizzas are fun – if you prepare some ingredients then she can put together her pizza. She may use ingredients that make the pizza look nice rather than taste nice, but then eat it anyway because it's 'hers'.
- Another thing my mum used to do is sit down in front of us and eat a snack – something like an apple which she cut up in front of us. Me and my sister would get curious and want to share.

gemma

A lot of children do go through this phase, and the usual advice is not to worry too much. Try to provide her with meals that are largely familiar, but with one or two unfamiliar things, and encourage her to try one mouthful of new things – but don't force her to eat anything she doesn't like. Also, if she sees that you're eating and enjoying the 'novel' foods, she may well be more inclined to try them. Another possibility is getting her involved in preparing food: most kids really enjoy 'cooking' (even if that just means arranging things on plates or stirring stuff), and feeling involved often encourages them to be more adventurous in their tastes.

Oh, another thing: if kids don't like the look of vegetables, including them in 'hidden' forms in pasta sauce, bolognese etc. can be helpful, and a lot of kids will very happily eat pasta with a basic 'red sauce', particularly if they're allowed to sprinkle cheese on top! In fact, encouraging kids to garnish food with a dollop of cream or a sprinkle of cheese or some crunchy croutons (for soup) can often be a good way of getting them to at least try it!

sushidog

When my son's old enough he'll definitely be enlisted in cooking – he's only two now, so there's a limit to what he can do, but he does REALLY enjoy helping to stir or pour ingredients together (e.g. I weigh out the flour, sugar, butter, milk etc. into separate bowls and then get him to mix *this* one with *that* one, and so on).

I can heartily recommend *How to get your kid to eat (but not too much)*. The basic advice in there would be to make a nice variety of healthy food, set it all out on the table, then have everyone sit together to eat. Each person can take what they want. If one toddler fills up on nothing but bread then that's no problem; over time, as the choice is always there, and they see the other members of the family enjoying the variety, they'll gradually start to try more stuff.

Cooking something separate specifically for the children is not a helpful path to start down: my brother in law is 34, and when we stay with my parents in law he still has to have a separate special meal cooked just for him. No way am I getting myself into that situation! If my son (who's two and a bit) is hungry at a time when the rest of us aren't eating, he just gets something like toast or yoghurt; otherwise, he shares whatever we're having.

vicky l

My son's favourite meal is currently spag bol, probably because he can turn himself bright orange after smearing the sauce all over his face.

When he is being picky I normally just lay out a bunch of little things and leave him to it: sliced banana, raisins, bread with spready cheese, apple bits, rice cakes, carrots (and if I'm feeling brave a yoghurt too!)

sa

I second the home-made macaroni cheese, I used to go crazy for that when I was little, still do, in fact.

Mum says there are things that I used to eat with gusto as a baby but I won't touch now. Apparently I adored beetroot and would eat a ton of the stuff, but the thought of eating it now makes me want to throw up!

A friend of mine has a kid that won't touch *any* vegetables: she ended up making potato patties and mixing very small amounts of carrots in, then breadcrumbing them or battering them and cooking. It worked for a good few months until he found an 'orange bit' and realised what she was up to!

phoenix 1979

Put stuff on your own plate and tell her she's not allowed it? Sometimes contrariness works in our favour...

Or, if she's getting a balanced diet (some veg, some carbohydrate and some protein) in what she will eat then just give her that repeatedly. One of my cousins ate nothing but white rice, sweetcorn and tuna for four years and he's grown up to be 6ft 2 and went to university, so clearly neither brain nor body were damaged by the boringness of his diet.

nicky s

KIDS' CLOTHING

Without wishing to sound tight-fisted, I have never understood the point in spending vast amounts of money on children's clothes. They'll be outgrown in a matter of months and will, likely as not, be subjected to all kinds of rough treatment. My

daughter usually has three or four nice dresses at
any one time, and apart from that it's trousers and
T-shirts/jumpers all the way. I quite often buy her
clothes from Asda or Tesco, but also M&S,
Mothercare, Bhs and Next. Not that it matters
really, because the same problems seem to repeat
themselves no matter where I look or how many
zeroes there are on the price tags.

The first objection I have to the current crop of
girlswear is the fact that it is just about impossible to
find any trousers at all that don't have horrid, bootcut
flared legs, and increasingly hard to find anything with
any sort of length in the body – i.e. not hipsters. In
my opinion these styles look bad enough on style-
challenged 14-year-olds experimenting to find their
'look'! Why the hell are we supposed to dress toddlers
in them too?!

This leads me to my next point: the fact that, as
soon as they have grown out of traditional baby
clothes, little girls are apparently supposed to start
dressing like teenagers. I can just about handle crop
tops, at least in the summer, but pelmet skirts, heeled
boots and hipsters for pre-teens are just wrong! The
worst example of this distressing trend that I have seen
is a PVC miniskirt in age 5–6 years size. I admit I am a
little old-fashioned in that I prefer children to look
like children, but I can't believe anyone in their right
mind wants them to look like prostitutes!

Fair enough, the PVC was an extreme case, but
even more appropriately styled garments are ruined by
tacky slogans. Call me a fuddyduddy if you will, but I
don't really want people studying my daughter's
bottom to see what the message on the back of her
jeans says, but it's either this or horrible 'designer'
labels which – sorry if this sounds pejorative – just

look common. Why is it so difficult to find plain things these days?

Because I was ill at the weekend and unable to do the shopping I needed to do, the clothing situation had become critical by this morning so I went to Asda on my lunch break intent on stocking up. Admittedly I did manage to find a beautiful coat, unspoiled by the usual 'fun' fur that looks grubby and cheap after just a few days of wear, but other than that I was pretty much drawing a blank to find anything suitable. In desperation I resorted to checking the boys' range. Not only did I find some perfectly suitable cord trousers in neutral colours, similar to the ones in the girls' section but without the tarty belts and flared ends, they also turned out to be half the price of the girls' equivalent! I will be looking in the boys' aisle more regularly in future – thank God my daughter is not old enough to mind!

sarah malaise

I get my daughter's clothes off eBay, I highly recommend it.

tooth_fairy

I agree little girls should be dressed like little girls. Try H&M, they are quite trendy without being tacky, and quite good value too.

whatsthestory

God, my friend has this exact problem with her two-year-old daughter. She suggests Matalan! Whenever anyone gripes about baby clothes, she says Matalan. They're cheap, casual, not too fussy, plenty of basics.

They may not last as long as something from more expensive stores, but for £2 for a pair of jeans, or £5 for a coat, do you really care? No, I say!

ugl

I saw a little girl of perhaps 5 a while back, wearing a mesh T-shirt (lined on the body, but mesh arms) with bondage straps on it. It wouldn't have looked out of place at a Goth club or even a fetish club.

Is there a branch of the National Childbirth Trust in your area? They sometimes have nearly-new sales, which can be fantastic, although your daughter might be a bit old for them now.

My mum used to get loads of stuff from Clothkits for me when I was young: corduroy dresses and trousers, T-shirty stuff etc., very hard-wearing, and not expensive. I agree that designer stuff for kids is a waste of money (saw an ad on TV yesterday for kids' clothes at Debenhams, with stuff for 5- and 6-year-olds at £50 and up; what's the point of spending that much when they're going to grow out of it in six months?), and I do hate seeing little children in teen-age gear. What happened to childhood?

sushidog

I totally agree on all points! My daughter is only nine weeks old so I have all this to come. She's already got a pair of flared trousers... what does a tiny baby need with flared trousers?

It's not much better in the boys' section. There's far less choice, most of the T-shirts have skater or gang-type designs all over them, and you're pretty much confined to jeans and T-shirts for them.

Don't even get me started on the sizing of lots of these things... my 19-month-old is still wearing 6–9 and 9–12-month trousers because they're freakishly long (he *is* kinda short in the leg dept, but not *that* short) and shirts he's still wearing 12–18 months and with tons of room still in them, and he's an average size. Primark are in another world with their sizes.

And the price of kids' shoes is another sore point. £25 for a pair of shoes that last eight weeks if you're lucky? Daylight robbery. My son has width H, so it's not like I can even get them from anywhere cheaper.

ladyynara

I confess I raid the boys' aisle at Asda fairly often for T-shirts and hoodies! I can fit in 12–14-year-old-boy-sized tops from George, and the designs are quite funky. And I'm a 28-year-old woman!!

lozette

There seem to be two genders in pre-teens: boys, and bratz. The next step will be getting breast enhancements for pre-teens or fake pubic hair (shudder). Luckily for me I have boys, which means I'll be less bothered by the current obsession with sexing up our little girls.

vf

When I last had to buy kids' stuff as a present, I ended up in the boys' section in Debenhams.

Is a trawl through a selection of decent charity shops worth a go? I go for me when I don't want what's currently fashionable, so I guess it would work for kids too, though I've never tried it myself.

lisa g

What about secondhand shops or charity shops? You can often get really good stuff for next to nothing.

Ivor

I used to love Ladybird clothes when I was young – and I wasn't a girly girl. The brand is owned by Woolies now. Also, have you thought of looking in catalogues? Kays etc. might do some plain things at reasonable prices – although buying from catalogues can be a pain.

jj

A CHILD-MINDER'S PLEA

Having been a childcarer for 11 years, trained and worked with every age and in a huge range of environments, I know some of the tricks. But there are some simple things that parents can do to make such a huge difference to the relationship between the carer, child and parent/guardians relationships.

PLEASE talk to your childcarer. Sadly, chances are they'll never be as good, nor wish to be, as the role parents have with their children, but it's been shown time and again that consistency is about the only thing that reliably helps children to settle in new environments, with new carers and new routines. TELL your carer how you do things: yes they may have had training in childcare, but you are the expert on your child – share that wisdom. Be open to suggestions from the carer, but tell them how you do things and why: it makes everyone's life a lot easier and the child's happier.

Please, I beg of you, share with the carer, no matter how little relevance you think it may have; child development is a many-faceted event and the more information and understanding the carer has, the more appropriately and seamlessly they can mirror the family procedures and activities for your benefit. You're paying them to help you, so equip them with the ability to understand WHY things happen the way they do.

Before employing a new carer:

- Get references, get written contact details including a home address, get an idea of their personal commitments and any medical con- ditions that will affect their ability to work reli- ably, get a photocopy of some photo ID – visa/ passport if applicable, get copy of their union card/Enhanced (to work with young people and vulnerable adults) Criminal Records Bureau check (CRB) within two years of date or a local area police check, get a good understanding of their limitations, boundaries, flexibility and abilities.
- Talk them through your children's interests, hobbies, personal development, and what you want from a childcarer. Tell them what you want from them, but be understanding that the first one you meet may not be appropriate or willing

to take on the job. Find out if they want the job. Offer them a cooling-off period if they accept, offer an introduction to the children and a trial visit while you are in the same environment.

- Talk through the intricate aspects of the family routine and don't skip bits about the correct type of biscuit allowed – knowing the carer isn't up to speed on the small things just causes lots of problems for the child.

- Discuss your method for disciplining your children. 'I don't do any' is just not true. If you tell your child and it responds instantly to you, super, but how would you like any problems to be dealt with? The carer will need to have tighter discipline in some areas than you as this isn't their child, and they can't make decisions that you'd not consider much but act upon – if he won't go to ballet, is it ok for him to miss it?

- Upon establishing a job spec and role with your carer keep a good line of communication with the carer, the child and any other family members who need to be involved. Give feedback consistently, good or bad, and PLEASE give them updates on vital information with the child – if it's a school-avoidant stage, tell them that its because of the boy in the class being a problem; if it's reaching hormonal swings stage, tell them so they can respond appropriately.

- Keep them abreast with family circumstances and changes – if Dad walked out last night, chances are the kids might need supporting the next day.

- Keep your child involved in the carer's appraisal: What do they think? What would they like to change?

- Finally, if things are at crisis point with your

children and you want some support or new ways of dealing with situations, ask your carer; if they're appropriately trained they will have ideas, and after watching you interact with your children will have observations that might help. The distance they have helps them see the cracks as well as the family glue. It doesn't need to hit Supernanny stage before change can be implemented.

Please, I'm sure this is all obvious, but, TALK TO YOUR CARER!

ebee

PARENTAL LEAVE

Has anyone had experience of taking this at work? My husband wants to take some time off to help me out at home as I have severe PND, and he hasn't got any holidays left. He's only taken time off so far when either he's been ill or I've been ill, so I haven't had any extra general help, which is what my doctor has told me I need.

He's worried about telling work that he wants some time to help me out, in case it makes him more likely to be made redundant, so I've not asked him to do this – he's offered.

Any advice and/or useful websites that he can read, as we don't actually know anything about how it actually works? We do know it's unpaid,

which will be a strain as we can't afford it, but some things are more important than money.

anna

You have to take it in blocks of a week: there's a limit of something like three or four weeks a year, and strictly it has to be for care of a child (so make sure he phrases it that way to his employer, rather than for taking care of you). You can find out more about it here: http://www.dti.gov.uk/er/parental_leave.htm

vicky l

A SENSITIVE SUBJECT

How do you best emphasise to a child to tell you if someone abuses them, be it sexually, physically or emotionally? How do you explain when they are to know when something is 'wrong' without scaring them or giving them too much detail?

I remember explicitly having the 'don't get into a car with a stranger' conversations and that sort of thing; however, abuse doesn't always come from the unknown (in fact this is less common than from a known source).

My daughter is nearly four and I don't have memories to draw on as to how to approach the subject with her with sensitivity and a lack of

hysteria. I want to be able to get her to understand that she should always tell me or her father
if someone touches her inappropriately or hurts
her. At the same time, though, I am aware that
children at this age sometimes lie (not from
malice, but just because they do) – how do I
make sure that she wouldn't lie about something
like that?

How did your parents deal with this issue?
How do you deal with it with your own children?

tooth_fairy

I've always talked about where it's okay to touch/not
to touch with my children and tried to introduce that
from situations that occurred naturally, and said to
them that if anyone touches them or talks to them in a
way they don't like, hurts them or makes them
uncomfortable, they should tell the person to stop and
tell Mummy or other trusted grown-up as soon as
they can. I don't think it's hysteria-inducing to teach
them to be safe and try to learn to protect themselves:
far better to talk about stuff. There are books about
things like bad touch/good touch and good secrets/
bad secrets that you can get which can be helpful.

rainbow

The main advice given is to teach children they are
allowed to say no, and loudly. That you will believe
them and not make them be nice to anyone if they
don't like that person, even if that person is known to
them.

http://www.saferchild.org/listen.htm
http://www.saferchild.org/teach.htm

http://www.saferchild.org/whocan.htm
(the last is mostly about saying no to peer pressure.)

blue_cat

SNORING

This is driving me absolutely batty. Can anyone help?

My other half snores. This is not a problem if I'm asleep – he doesn't make enough noise to wake me up. But if he goes to sleep first, or if I wake in the night I can't get (back) to sleep because of his snoring. I'm losing at least an hour's sleep every night because of this, often more, and I'm going nuts.

Does anyone know any ways to stop/prevent snoring? Making him turn over doesn't work any more – it used to, but now he snores on his side as well as his back. Kicking him doesn't work, and eventually wakes him up and makes him cross. Earplugs don't work: they're un-comfortable and don't block the noise anyway. He can sleep without snoring; it's just that more and more (or so it seems) he doesn't.

dorian

You poor thing!!

Go to Boots. They sell nose clips that can help, and also a liquid that I think he gargles with. Definitely talk to the pharmacist – they should be able to help you.

Does he need to lose weight? That can cause snoring.

cookwitch

VASECTOMY

Advice on vasectomy aftercare?

anna

Did they give him any painkillers? Tell him to take them. If they didn't, OldBloke took ibuprofen (which was prescribed) and the occasional paracetamol, but avoided the stronger painkillers because he's a MAN. Or something.

Keep an eye on the wounds – OB's vasectomy was a month ago and he got an infection within a couple of days that still hasn't quite healed.

k425

A bag of frozen peas – wrap the bag in a teatowel – you don't want something frozen touching the body in case you get ice burns.

darth tigger

MOVING IN TO-GETHER

I'm about to move into a house with my bloke and I've never lived with a partner before, at least not in a whole 'properly getting a house together' way, rather than just sleeping there every night for months. Any tips as to how to make sure it works? I know from experience that living with someone else can be hard work, so I just thought I'd ask what problems people have had that I might anticipate and how they dealt with them.

kk

I've never lived with a partner, though I have lived with plenty of friends and fellow students. The only advice I can really give is to discuss any problems either of you has, and don't let anything stew, it'll only get worse and niggle at you. Good luck

vgl

Work out a housework rota. It'll save a lot of 'but I do all the xxxx' or the 'you never do the xxx!' type of arguments.

cookwitch

Again, from living with friends/housemates rather than with a boyfriend or partner; have a long chat to start with about house rules – things like cleaning/housework rotas (if one of you wants the place to be made spotless twice a week, and the other feels a quick Hoover every other month is fine, it will cause tension... financial stuff (Who pays for what? Does everything come out of a joint account? Do you contribute equally, or according to your incomes?), rules about inviting friends over (if one of you expects a month's notice in writing of any visitors, and the other wants to invite people back after the pub to stay for a few days, you're in trouble) and so on.

Also, it's worth making sure you each have some space of your own, either by having an area in the house (study, shed, whatever) that is yours and yours alone, or by agreeing that, say, on Wednesday nights you'll do things separately, whether that's staying home with a good book or going out with other friends. Having a bit of independence (whether it's a couple of hours a week out with other people, or three days a week locked in separate rooms, depending on what suits you!) can really help!

sushidog

Not lived with a boyfriend myself but that sounds like very good advice. I think I'd add that talking about this stuff before you even move in is probably a better idea than doing it once you have, because otherwise, y'know, you'll be tired after moving, then work, and you'll drift into a pattern of housework/domestic stuff without quite realising that you haven't explicitly agreed anything.

sk

Talk about timescales. I was bought up to do all chores first, then you have all the time for play: the Mr was bought up differently. This has led to the odd clash: for example I expect the Mr to take the rubbish out as soon as it needs doing. He is quite happy to do it when he's ready. This has led to more discussions than I can think. We now compromise.

Keep talking, it's the only way to get things done, never drag out arguments and try not to leave the house angry.

jules

Explicit discussions and agreement about how to split housework, tidiness levels, finances... and anything else that either of you have ever gotten irritated with previous flatmates about. Little things like how kitchen cupboards are arranged and how often the sheets get washed can lead to SCREAMING RAGE at times.

I also very much second sushidog's comment about ensuring that you have separate time/space. After living with my partner for three years, *finally* with New House I have a room that is Mine. I don't sleep in it, but I have a desk in there, and my sewing machine and knitting stuff and a couple of bookcases, and a futon that is a sofa for if I have people round and don't want to be in the living room, but is also a bed for when it becomes the spare room. And it's *great* and has made me enormously happy and reduced my stress levels noticeably. So yeah – if you can't manage that, then another option is to agree, say, that every so often each of you can have the house to yourself for the evening.

Also, you may want to discuss what you both

expect in terms of socialising together – whether you'll be offended if you're ever excluded from anything the other does, or whether you'd be surprised if you were ever invited along (or, more likely, somewhere in between. Finances are relevant here as well – if one of you can afford more socialising than the other, whether the better-off one wants to sub the worse-off one sometimes, or all the time, or never.

Given that you've got studying to do, probably talking about what you need/expect in terms of quietness/support/cups of tea would be useful as well.

I know people who have explicit conflict-resolution agreements (although I don't myself) – e.g. they've agreed that if they get into a row, they'll take 30 minutes apart to calm down before discussing the issue and trying to find a compromise/solution. Depends how much trouble you have dealing with arguments/disagreements – if it's a difficult area then agreements like that can be handy, I think.

jk

Have you thought about opening a joint bank account? The way we did it was to work out how much rent and bills (including food) would come to per month, then split that between us in a way we were happy with (he started out paying more cos he earned more, but it's since evened out for other reasons), and pay that amount in on a standing order, straight after payday. It should mean you make a conscious decision about how much each of you is contributing (rather than the person who happens to open the bill being the one who pays), and the money's always available to pay bills cos it's sitting in a dedicated pot. Plus it's kinda nice to have a joint fund of money for things like takeaway and meals out, so you don't have to split the bill or take it in turns and worry about how fair that ends up being. And if you set all your bills up on direct debit, you never need to worry about them, as it all works automatically.

gj

If you like some chores and not others then a rota/ agreed split is definitely a good idea, otherwise you may end up doing the stuff you don't mind and the stuff you don't like doing. It worked out very nicely for me with the last fella I lived with, as we found that the chores split very handily. He did all the cooking because he liked it and I don't, and all the grocery shopping because he didn't mind that (and it made sense since he was the one cooking) and I hate it; whereas I did all the cleaning, laundry and washing up because I don't mind that and knew that, because he was messier than me, I'd end up doing it anyway.

A joint account is very handy for covering the grocery shopping: if it all comes out of the joint account then you can be sure you're paying for it equally. Ironically (in an I-can-laugh-about-it-now kind of way) aforementioned fella and I lived together for a year before he finally got around to sorting out the joint account. He then dumped me three days later.

caroline

I think it's all been covered. Just to add my voice to the masses... what happens in our house is:

- Whoever cooks a meal doesn't have to wash up.
- We do our laundry separately (I do mine routinely, he does his when he needs to, so we don't try to combine).
- I feel like I do more of the housework, but that's probably because I have a lower 'messiness' threshold than he does. But he makes up for it by blitzing the bathroom/dining room when we need to clean up specially for something, so I feel it evens out.

It doesn't really matter who does what as long as you're both happy. If you're not, you'll have to say something. Our arrangements evolved from my living with him temporarily before it was permanent, so we both kinda figured out what the other didn't mind doing.

lannie

I must admit that we didn't really have a Plan when we moved in together. We seem to just have fallen into what works for us – neither of us is particularly messy, nor are we scarily tidy, and the division of labour mostly balances out overall.

Stuff like laundry, taking the rubbish out, sorting the recycling, cooking and doing the dishes gets done by whoever notices it first. He mostly Hoovers (I don't like doing it), I mostly clean the bathroom and the kitchen. None of which are we fastidious about – as long as it's clean I don't mind if it doesn't sparkle.

The OH is allergic to the idea of a joint account for some reason, so stuff gets paid for separately but I don't particularly mind – it's not a huge issue for me. The one thing that really does make a difference is something that he's taught me to do and that his parents instilled in him – to say 'thank you' even for the most mundane stuff, like making dinner.

sera_squeak

Make sure you talk as you sort things out, and keep talking. If you or he has a poor memory (I have a brain like a sieve) make notes of what you agreed and any outstanding issues.

There is a handy page here – http://www.advice-now.org.uk/go/livingtogether/index – which has information about the legal side of moving in together, and a document called a Living Together Agreement. Even if you don't actually make one properly, it's an excellent way to look at all the really serious issues connected with this kind of move.

If there is anything he does that you have noticed really gets on your nerves, it will be worse when you live together. Discuss things rather than hoping they will improve on their own. Also, look at how much time you expect to spend together, or doing specific things. Some people treat 'time spent in the same building' as the equivalent of 'time spent With My Partner', even if they spend all their time attached to a computer screen and do not speak to you. Others would prefer to spend dedicated 'date' time together several times a week and then not feel obliged to be in every night. If either of you has hobbies or activities that take up your evenings and weekends, that's also relevant. Also consider ideas about how much sex/ intimate time you would ideally have; this can be quite different when you move in with someone compared to when you don't sleep together every night and thus have to take your chances when they arise.

Work out how you will cope with unexpected

problems: a window got broken; the fridge or wash-ing-machine has died; there is water spurting from the kitchen taps which will not be stopped; you have no hot water. Who organises a repair? Where does the money come from? What happens if you think the ratty old sofa needs a new cover, or a pile of cushions, and he thinks it doesn't? What if he wants a new light-fitting in the bathroom and you're fine with the old one? Working out how you might handle deci-sions like this is helpful.

Yfk

Keep the money separate. Agree what you will pay for communally, and stick to that. Apart from that, keep your money separate from his. This is really really important. It means you don't control his spending, and nor do you feel he controls yours. It means that you still respect each other as financially independent adults. It means if you choose to spend money on him, or vice versa, it is a gift, and can be viewed as such. Money is at the root of nearly all break-ups, once you get to the living-together stage.

juggzy

HUBCAPS

If you don't want to lose your hubcaps (not necessary with alloys) then use a couple of cable ties to secure the hubcap to the wheel hub.

silvernik

BO

A friend of mine doesn't have a very good sense of smell, which leads to him having a bit of a body odour issue. Sometimes it's fine, but sometimes – if it's hot and he's been on the Tube, for instance – it's quite unpleasant. I don't think he uses deodorant, maybe because he thinks it's bad for the environment – he's very green. Is there any way I can talk to him about it tactfully, or should I just come right out with it?

hk

If he's worried about the environment, Lush do some good deodorants. Maybe buy him some Lush goodies, including the deodorants... give it a few days, then ask how they're getting along. Did you like the stuff? How about those deodorants, they're a bit different aren't they? How're you finding them? Oh, you're not using them, how come? Well, the thing is X, the reason I got you the package is because, with it being summer and all, I think you could do with a little deodorant. I don't want to embarrass you, but you're a good mate and it's a shame.

Oh God, I don't know.

emma-leigh owen

How about suggesting a nice relaxing bath/shower when they have come to see you (separately or to-gether) and then passing over the deodorant after you have used it?

Sometimes I have had to tell people that they smell, usually after a club when my inhibitions are down thanks to alcohol I will admit; generally they take it pretty well and go and wash! That very much depends on the character of the whiffy person though. In my experience people would rather know about it than not.

Good luck, but whatever you do don't let something like this carry on – it'll be worse to deal with it in the future as it will become a much larger issue for you and your friend.

am

Most sprays are CFC-free these days anyway! Lush do some solid deodorants which are really nice, so perhaps one of them could be tactfully included in a box of other Lush goodies...?

janet mcknight

Having a husband with an incredibly poor sense of smell, I know exactly what you mean. I tend to say something about the heat, to cushion it a little, and also because I'd hate to put the idea into his head that he smells all of the time (just not true). Then mention that, after a long day, none of us is especially sweet-smelling, but his smell is a little overpowering.

My bloke uses unscented deodorant that is environmentally friendly too.

dw

SPECIAL TREATS FOR A LOVELY BLOKE

What are some cheap/free things I can do to make him feel really cared for? I'd love to shower him with gifts and take him out for dinner, but unfortunately that's just not in the budget!!!

mobilise

Love letters are a great idea. Breakfast in bed? with things you can feed each other? strawberries and stuff? Or a card made up from pictures you have cut out of magazines, newspapers and printed off the internet of all the lovely things you would like to give him, or things that make you think of him? A sort of 'You are so fabulous, these things remind me of you, and our relationship'?

nb

As you probably know it's the actions that count, the intention, rather than how much you've shelled out. Whenever I've been skint, I'll make a picnic and take them to the park. Yummy food (and you don't necessarily have to cook, you can just get some nice cheese, olives etc.), nice bottle of wine, sitting under a tree in the park, pamper him with your affections.

liese

You could make little trinket things – like a friendship bracelet or a little origami 'thing' for his desk. You can make a simple friendship bracelet by twisting or plaiting different-coloured threads. It's not much, but it's the thought that counts!

gemma

A long and attentive massage can be a wonderful gift. It doesn't have to cost anything at all, although you might want to get some massage oil.

When I was living away from my partner and didn't have any money, I used to make him endless compilation tapes with hand-done labels, and draw him lots of pictures and cards. We used to leave each other notes in stupid places (inside sandwiches, stuck inside note books... and I once picked up a chunk of stone he'd found me on a beach to find 'a chip off the old bloke' written on a Post-It note underneath).

Sending him mail might also be nice: someone once promised to send me a postcard every day for a week, which I thought was ever so sweet. Depending on where he works, you might be able to send stuff to him at work, too. Things to make him smile.

tb

Cheapest thing in the world: just tell him. It doesn't seem like much and I know the urge to pretty it up with a present or a special gesture, but think about it – when you've been on the receiving end, which meant more: the presents or the person you love saying 'Thank you' and 'I love you'?

caroline

How about writing him some promissory notes for various nice things: a foot rub, a massage, a blow-job, taking his turn to do the washing-up, whatever he's likely to enjoy! He can then 'cash in' his tokens whenever he likes.

sushidog

Arrange a surprise.

Idea (may not suit your sensibilities): Locate park. Locate picnic rug. Pick his and your favourite sandwich fillings. Buy nice bread and fruit. Acquire bubbles, balloons, Frisbees etc. (pound shop?) Acquire sunny weekend afternoon. Take food and rug and playthings to park. Have picnic. If necessary, ban discussion of the heavy stuff, and keep it focused on how much you care about each other and enjoy each other's company.

If this appeals but you want more, try the romantic-bathroom trick: candles, optional rose petals/deliciously scented bath products, and so on, and inveigle him into the bath/shower with you. This requires a largish bath or shower, of course.

The point is the thoughtfulness and the surprise.

ljk

Have you any arty/crafty skills? Maybe you could knit him a sweater, or sew him a shirt, or write a favourite poem in calligraphy, or carve him a paperweight, or write him a story, or paint him a picture, or grow him a rose, or some such.

dorian

ENGINEERING

The only two things an engineer ever needs are gaffer tape and WD40. One gets things moving when they're stuck and the other stops things moving when they're loose.

silvernik

HOW DO YOU GO ABOUT FINDING A PARTNER?

If you really want a partner (or another partner if you're poly), what steps do you take?

You see, I'm a bit of a freak: I'm not only happy single, but I actively prefer it. But I understand that most people in our society want to be in relationships. Many people, if they find themselves single, are really unhappy about this situation. So, if you are or have ever been one of those people, what do/did you do? I mean, just sitting around feeling sorry for yourself because there are no suitable partners out there or nobody fancies you is certainly one option, but I'm sure that some people are more assertive than that. Do you use dating agencies? Ask your friends to set you up with people? Take up activities to meet new people? What? And what has worked? Has anybody ever gone looking for a partner and found one (as opposed to just happening to meet the right person at the right moment?)

livre d'or

I met my partner at an anti-Valentines party for the militantly single. I would recommend asking a friend to organise one.

sarah malaise

Previously, I've used gaydargirls.com (more to meet people generally) and have been set up via friends. A lot of couples I know met online. I find that if I was lonely enough or bored enough, I'd go out on dates and generally try. But for the most part I was enjoying the single life until I was lucky enough to get back together with the girl I love.

how_i_lie

Generally, I do internet dating. I have never met anyone through friends or via bars/parties etc. I even met the guy I had my first kiss with (aged 18) via a Lonely Hearts ad in Select magazine!

lozette

If I was looking right now, I'd probably try online equivalent of Lonely Hearts. Though I do kind of fancy speed dating!

tamaranth

Well, I have...

- Gone to evening classes and met someone, but he was married.
- Met someone at work, but he was married.
- Done internet dating and met lots of very strange people and one wonderful person who was even single, until his wife came back.
- Joined Dateline and met lots of extremely strange people, some perfectly pleasant people, and one utter weirdo who stalked me.
- Joined the SCA and found lots of lovely, fanciable, smart, funny people, all of whom are married, and one who is single but was only interested in a quick shag.
- Met a couple of people online and had enjoyable, if short, relationships that just haven't worked out.

pp

All my partners in the last five years have been people with whom I was 'just good friends' beforehand, and whom I then decided it was OK to fancy after all.

Partners are lovely (and very useful sometimes!) but I can survive quite happily on my own as well and I'm generally far more productive! I can't say I've ever had the Bridget Jones Must-Find-Eligible-Man feeling. I have a lot of very good friends so I never feel lonely.

ks

All of my major relationships came about when I wasn't looking. I have gone to singles dances, not for the looking part, just for the dancing part. I was very content being single, though the last few years would have liked to have someone, but it was no big deal. Joining activities is good, meeting through work or friends sometimes works. Online dating and meeting these days seems a lot more common. I met my guy online through a mutual friend.

ivor

CAR ADVICE

If you should ever lock your keys inside your car with the engine running, you can stop it by holding a flat shoe over the exhaust pipe – the car will backfire and the engine will cut out.

moggy

OIL

Never check the oil level in your car when your engine is warm or your car is not on level ground.

silvernik

MOTORBIKE INSURANCE

I have a motorbike! Now I need to insure it, so I can practise on a road. Does anyone have any recommendations? Bonus points for anything a) net-based that will b) also work on Firefox, as I'm at work and can't really phone round.

Does anyone have any experience of the women-only insurance people (and any names of such companies), so I can look there also?

bee

Most of my biker friends (and I have *lots*) seem to like www.carolenash.com.

ramtops

I would recommend going with a bike-only or bike-specialist insurer. They are much better in the event of an accident than the usual ones – says the one who's still fighting two bike accident cases.

Hubs used Bennetts bike-only insurers. Also have a look at joining something like the BMF – they do legal advice and all kinds of stuff. WELL worth it. Honest (you can join online).

cookwitch

I've used Diamond for car insurance before, and let me just say, they're shite. Really really shite. And expensive. I much prefer Direct Line nowadays.

vgl

Diamond were my saviours, whereas Direct Line on the face of it appeared to be good but then turned out to be rubbish and refused to insure me because I was under 25 and my car had alloy wheels.

sara

Carole Nash!! Most of the big women-only companies don't insure bikes.

My bike's been off the road for ages, but I always used Carole Nash, and never had any problems.

desiring cairo

I used Diamond for my woman-only insurance, and only stopped because a man wanted to be insured on my car, selfish bugger. When I got hit by an elderly loonie, they were great and sorted it! Not sure if they cover bikes though...

littlebluefish

eBike insurance (Google it!) gave me a darn fine quote!

kimkali

TAXI SAFETY

Unlicensed taxi cabs seem like an easy option when you're staggering home late from the centre of town; however, the number of assaults on women is really worrying.

If you text the word HOME to 60835, you'll get a text back with the phone numbers for one black cab number and two local licensed mini-cab firms.

You can open an account with a company such as Addison Lee (www.addisonlee.com) who'll charge you monthly.

Make sure the cab you get into is the one you've booked, check that the driver has your name, and sit in the back, behind the driver.

moggy

FIRST PERIODS

Do you remember the first time?

This post is being brought to you by the godawful pain in my lower back. When did you get your first period? How did you feel? Who did you tell, and what did they say?

I got mine at nearly 14, which my friend reck-
ons is really late, but what I suspect might be a
little bit weird is that when I told my mum, she
actually cheered, picked me up and swung me
around and enthused about how fantastic it was
that I was a Woman and stuff. And that did feel
good. The enthusiasm infected me, even though
I actually felt like all my insides were about to fall
out. But I know other people who told their
mums in fear and trembling, and the mums
blushed and fidgeted and snapped something
about towels and keeping yourself fresh, and that
was that. Maybe that's just an Irish thing.

bluedevi

I think I was 14, or very nearly, so quite late I
suppose. It was while staying with a friend on a
country break, and I remember having a little smile to
myself about it but not telling anyone.

starmix

I got mine on November the 4th 1992, and I would
have been 12 that year. I remember the stomach
cramps the day before, but I didn't realise for a couple
of days that what was happening to me was actually a
period because the stuff was kind of thickish and
brown and didn't look like blood.

My mum was fine with it, and she explained the
use of towels and I felt more womanly and special,
like it was an important rite of passage and I already
had the smugness of knowing I would have an
excuse at least once a month to skip PE and intimid-
ate men. Which all means that I will have been

having periods for 12 years, during which time I've missed only one.

rainsinger

I think I can win hands down on 'times you really don't want to start your period'.

I was at my Grandfather's funeral. We had been to the church and we were back at my Gran's house for the family get-together afterwards, and I was sitting on the stairs and my Mum said 'I think you should go to the bathroom'. I did and soaked through my pants and my tights was this brown manky gunge. I was so embarrassed that it happened at the funeral. Oh yeah, and it was 3rd June 1988, when I was 12.

elizabeth

July 13, 1987. I was 11. It was my little brother's birthday. I was a bit pissed off, actually. I was expecting it because my family (my grandmother and aunt, who were both nurses) were always very open about bodily functions. There was no 'You're a woman!' or celebration or anything, just practical advice. I think I preferred it that way, since I saw it as the beginning of a lifelong nuisance.

offensive_mango

I was 12 when it happened, which is now half of my life ago.

The first time my mum had tried to tell me about such things was when she was drunk and didn't manage to tell me in a particularly good way, and I was scared and ran to the back room and found comfort in being near my bicycle.

Some time later than that, it was late at night and I couldn't sleep, and she gave me a leaflet from a magazine that either she or my grandmother had been reading, a magazine that may have been Woman's Weekly, or something like that. There had also been education at school and books and magazines that I'd read, although I never did understand the belt contraption they sometimes used in Judy Blume books.

On the day it happened in August, I called my mum into the bathroom and she asked me if I was sure and then gave me appropriate advice. The one thing that I remember being confused about at the time was why it didn't stop at night.

judith_crunch

I was 11 or 12 (and I don't think that's particularly early – I certainly wasn't the first of my friends) and I noticed it as I was about to leave for school. I was a bit embarrassed about telling my mum, but as the alternative was going to school and having to tell the school matron, I did tell her. Although I knew all about how these things happened, it was still a bit of a shock. It didn't hurt at all.

When I got back from school later that day, there was a big bunch of flowers in my room, which I found really embarrassing – especially as my little sister let on she knew what they were for, and I guessed my dad had been told too. I just wanted to get on with it in private. Actually, the flowers thing was odd, looking back, because before and since, periods were treated by my mother – and also by me to a degree – as something that need to be dealt with but not discussed. There was certainly no leaving towels or tampons in the bathroom – the towels my mum bought me were hidden at the back of my bottom drawer behind my school uniform.

For a couple of years I struggled with towels – they weren't the slimline things they are today, and the brand my mum bought me were 'shaped' and bulky. I dreaded having to use them far more than I dreaded my actual period. Eventually I managed to buy and figure out tampons, and I'd never go back now. Oh, and another horrible thing I remember about the towels was that I wasn't allowed to put them down the loo at home, and there was no bin, so I had to wrap them in loo roll and sneak into the kitchen to dispose of them. Ugh.

dozle

I think I was 13. I do remember it started when I was at home, and wearing a pair of (annoyingly) white dungarees. My mum and I were both calm and matter-of-fact about it – I'd read *Are you there God? It's me, Margaret*, and had asked my mum for a facts of life book★ several years earlier, so I knew all about it. I used tampons from the beginning – I suppose I must've had a supply in anticipation, because although my mum also used them, hers were the super-extramega sort, so not really stealable at that stage.

★We were in the local post office, which sold books, and I found the book I wanted (the Usborne Book Of Growing Up, or some such thing), took it up to her, and demanded she buy it for me. And then I wished that that technique worked for other books as well.

gj

I was 12. It happened one evening at home and I was too embarrassed to go and tell my mum, so far ages I walked in circles round my room with loo roll down my knickers getting more and more worked up. Eventually I went downstairs and stood in the living room doorway, where my mum and dad were watching TV, and went 'ummm, ummm, er, ummmm', prompting my mum to come out and speak to me on the stairs. I said 'I, er, think I've got my period' and she went 'oh, is THAT all it is?' and went and got me some towels and tampons from her room. That was the only conversation we ever really had about it. But my periods when I was younger were just hellish. They lasted ten days at a time, and I'd get through a super-plus tampon every two hours. Totally exhausting, and not at all like the Judy Blume books.

tb

It's not really late – just quite late. I know someone who didn't get theirs until they were 17. And someone else who never got hers.

Mine started when I was 11 – but I can't remember the first one, really. I know that may seem odd, but I had been told it was coming for so long beforehand that it was just a case of 'meh' when it finally came.

I know that I grew bosoms in about two weeks a few months later – I went from completely flat-chested to absolutely huge in no time. It was a bit peculiar really.

elethe

14. It was the last day of term before the Christmas holidays, and I was in a concert with the school orchestra. I stuffed paper towels down my knickers.

Mum had already (a year or two earlier) explained it all to me and bought me some towels, so when I got home I changed to them. It was about four hours before I got the nerve to tell her, but she was really matter-of-fact about it and said she'd get me more the next day, so there was always a plentiful supply in the house.

It was then several months before my next one, which I was somewhat relieved about – I could do without all that hassle too often! Sadly it later settled down to every four weeks or so. Still, you get used to it!

darth tigger

I don't remember exactly when it was – I think I was 12. I remember getting up in the night with what I thought was a stomach pain, and my mother telling me it might be my period. And I dreaded it. A day or two later, it was.

My mother insisted I use towels, too, though I don't know why. I nicked some of her tampons for a while until I could get my own.

I didn't get the 'rites of passage womanhood thing' at all. I sometimes wish I had – which does involve wishing my family's attitude to bodies all round had been healthier. Then maybe mine might have been healthier as well.

bee

I was only just 11... it wasn't a big deal! I think my Mum said something along the lines of 'Oh dear... well, you've got the next 40 years or so to endure...'

duckiemonster

Another probably weird thing – I found out all the basic facts of life when I was about four, because my little bro was on the way and I basically pestered the information out of both parents. I was working on both of them at once, so each of them still to this day (touchingly) thinks they were the first to tell me. Mum's version was entertaining but medical. Dad's involved a little story where the Egg goes skipping through the Fallopian Tube Woods, with a basket on her arm, and then runs into the Sperm of her Dreams...

I still had misconceptions, though. Mum said that because the blood is the same temperature as your body, you can't feel it, and this can cause embarrassing leaks etc. So I was surprised when I definitely could feel it.

bluedevi

I was 10 – it was about a month short of my 11th birthday, which is early, I think. I was still in the top year of junior school, and I don't know anyone else who started before they got to secondary. I noticed at about 10 in the morning but I was too embarrassed to tell my mother until the afternoon. She was terribly matter-of-fact about it, but she told my dad and he made some comment later on which I was really embarrassed about. This was April as well, and we did

swimming at school in the summer term and I remember having to lie to my teacher a couple of times
about why I couldn't swim (and at the time I was
amazed she believed me!).

wh

Er, around 12 I think. French lesson. Ironically, had
been having a conversation with the rest of my table
about who had 'started.' Wasn't desperately excited or
interested in it. Certainly didn't really make me feel
different or grown up or anything.

kauket

I can't remember for the life of me. My mum was
very practical, though, going through a book called
Have you started yet? with me. As with the How are
babies made? talk, I remember being revolted and
thinking afterwards that I was better off before I'd
found out about this stuff. Prissiness and denial – the
teenage Jo there!

jo

I was 12. It did a number on my hormones and I was
suicidal, but once I figured out why I wasn't so bad. I
knew the technical side, luckily – the benefits of
having a mother who was a bio teacher I guess.
However I had no idea of what it was actually like.

Had awful problems with cramps through my teens
and it wasn't until I first moved in with a bloke that I
found out it wasn't normal – I remember spending
Christmas morning sobbing in the foetal position on
the floor and him saying his other girlfriends hadn't

been anything like this. I was physically sick from the pain and I can now safely say it was worse than childbirth. It took two gynaecologists to diagnose adenomyosis, but the first explained why I couldn't use tampons without pain, let alone have intercourse. I had a relatively minor operation to fix that. The adeno was 'cured' by my first full-term pregnancy.

mjf

SPIKED DRINKS

You can get kits to test for drinks-spiking if you're concerned. Not tried using them, but I've seen them in Boots – £1.50 or something, usually displayed by the tills – shouldn't break the bank.

sea_of_flame

BARBIES

You can brush my hair, undress me everywhere...
   Did you have a Barbie when you were a bairn? What did you do with her, and what was your attitude to her? What is your attitude now?

Me, I didn't have one – I had a large army of Playmobil people, and when I say army they did often actually go to war against each other. But I understand that many people have Barbie stories to tell, and they're, um, interesting...

jo

I had a Princess Barbie something or other. It was a gift from Santa at my grandfather's bowling club Christmas party *shudder*. I put her over a lamp in a bid to heat her hair and straighten it. It seemed like a good idea at the time, but I managed to forget about where I'd left Barbie, melted her hair to her head and almost started a fire. The whole house smelled like melting synth hair and my mum hit the roof. My dad cut what was left of her hair into a fashionable crew cut with some nail scissors. She looked quite butch. I was never keen on dolls anyway.

pipistrellus

I had a Barbie, and I dressed her up and brushed her hair and did all the usual things. Gave one a fringe once – bad idea. Made mine ride My Little Ponies when they came out, and have relationships with teddy bears (I never had a Ken).

I also used to put them naked (didn't want to ruin the clothes!) in the middle of the road and sit in the front yard giggling, waiting for cars to run them over. My Barbies all had dented breasts... Oh, and I used to chew her feet cause they were all soft and squidgy, so my Barbies also all had misshapen and broken feet with bite marks around the ankles.

silke

I had a Barbie. I gave her a punk haircut and pierced her ears with dressmakers' pins. Did you know Barbie's head is slightly narrower than the length of a dressmakers' pin? The points ended up coming out the other side.

I think I much preferred my Strawberry Shortcake doll. Equally anatomically incorrect, but much friendlier.

myf

I didn't have a Barbie, but I had several Sindy dolls, which I thought were clearly superior and much less wet and silly. They got up to adventures (usually of the non-euphemistic kind) with my brother's various He-Man figures, even though the Sindys were about twice the height of the He-Men.

I was never much interested in dressing them up – they were just the actors in the adventure stories we played out, and they weren't even our preferred actors, because it was much harder to acquire/construct the props and sets that the stories demanded than it was with Lego people!

ej

I didn't have one as a child – but I have thousands of them stashed under my bed at my parents' house now. No room for them in London. I had a year or two of madness inspired by boredom (and deprivation as a child) and bought loads of the things. Don't know what came over me. (I also collected coins, Beanie Babies and silver – I think of them as my dragon years).

elethe

I did have a Sindy – but not until a lot later than my friends. She was actually a Snow White doll, but I bought a spare head at a Sindy Doll spares shop in Portsmouth and stuck it on the body. It had red hair and was beautiful – until I decided to make her a punk, transsexual, single mother Sindy and cut all her hair off. It doesn't grow back, you know.

(My brother hid his Action Man from me when he found out I was dressing it in dolls' clothes and using him as the 'before' to Sindy's 'after'.)

I didn't have official Sindy clothes – my grand-mother used to make them out of wool for me (and for my brother's Action Man – he had a lovely purple jumper as I recall).

elethe

I did have a Barbie, a Sindy, and many of the trappings, a house and a horse and stuff. Also Jem dolls (does anyone else remember them??) I think I am alone in actually liking and playing with them when I was little (embarrassment). All quite innocent stuff, actually. Never had any male dolls. Any other dolls than those (e.g. baby dolls etc.) scare the living day-lights out of me, still do. Had some clothes, and mam made some more clothes for me. It was all quite innocent. I fear that I am a freak...

bee

I had one Sindy, one Skipper (Barbie's little sister) and four flower fairies (one of whom was disabled due to a foot-chewing incident as described by Silke), and some sort of baby-shaped thing. They were a family: Sindy was the mum, Skipper was about 15 or 16, and

the flower fairies were about 12 or 13 and quads.
Skipper was hugely jealous because she had a completely flat chest, whereas all her little sisters had rather
nice curves and boobs.

The flower fairies were my favourites: Skipper
would sit around sighing about boys and Sindy
would be looking after the baby, so the flower fairies
would go off having adventures and learning to
rock-climb up my chest of drawers and stuff. And
they'd always wait for the disabled one and encourage her. (I thought the idea of being somewhere
where everything was giant-sized and you could
rock-climb up chests of drawers and use chairs like
climbing frames was so wicked that I nearly wrote
to Jim'll Fix It to ask whether he could design a
playground like that.)

Occasionally, Sindy would come along and tell
them off, or Skipper would come along and try and
join in their adventures. But Skipper was a bit of wuss,
and they'd all get annoyed with her for whining.

I also sewed clothes for them a lot.

la bias

I used to play with my mother's Barbies from the
1950s (original black and white swimsuits and all)
whenever I visited my grandmother. Apparently my
cousin and I exhibited some sort of undesirable behaviour towards the Barbies' hair when we were very
little, because both dolls had their hair each in one
braid tied firmly with white cotton thread. Eventually
the Barbie rule list included:

- No unbraiding the Barbies' hair.
- No losing the Barbies' plastic high heels in the

orange shag pile carpet where they could break the Hoover.
- No whacking each other with the Barbies.
- No playing 'Flying Barbie princess from outer space' outside the bedroom if grandfather is watching football.

easterbunny

I didn't have a Barbie, although unfortunately – given my general disdain of girly paraphernalia – I did once have a Sindy. Bleaugh! I think I gave her to someone who actually liked that kind of stuff.

I am a firm believer that TV etc. advertising encourages (nay enforces) a pink, cute, girly, dolly image on young females which results in an enforced mindset for the rest of their lives [lies?]; this is the same image that tells us that boys should play with guns. I could rant but...

am

WEEKENDS AWAY

It's my birthday in September, and rather than the usual big party with a bunch of friends, I'm hoping to have a weekend away with my partner. Can any of you recommend somewhere wonderful (in the UK) for us to go?

nurse_liz

Tintagel (or indeed anywhere in Cornwall) is beautiful. At the end of the season you should be able to get a cottage for a very reasonable sum. We stayed in Windmill just outside Padstow one time and it was easily within walking distance to Padstow, the beach and all sorts of places, whilst being wonderfully isolated too.

am

The Dungeon Ghyll hotel in Dungeon Ghyll, Cumbria (near Ambleside) is beautiful and is in such a lovely location.

tooth_fairy

York's lovely, if you've not been. My partner and I went a couple of years ago and stayed in a lovely B&B which did the BEST cooked breakfasts EVER. I think it was called the Holmwood House Hotel or something like that. It was lovely in any case! And there's loads of stuff to do – ghost walks, cathedrals, old quaint pubs, plenty of walks and museums, and the infamous Jorvik of course!

easternpromise

I absolutely adore The Rose and Crown in Snettisham, Norfolk. The food is incredible, the rooms are characterful and really luxurious, and the village is pretty. There's a huge stretch of beach a couple of miles away, but I wouldn't recommend going to it unless you have your own transport (it's a long walk)! The pub is about 15 miles from King's Lynn. I've been twice so far, and I'm considering booking it to celebrate my Mum's 70th birthday next year.

kate b

- Edinburgh: most beautiful city in the country (biased? Me?)
- Lavenham: very, very pretty village in Cambridgeshire (or perhaps it's Norfolk), very quiet, but with nice old hotels.
- New Forest: Hampshire – open spaces, horses, pretty villages, and the option of a daytrip to the Isle of Wight if you like.
- Glen Coe: One of my favourite places ever – stunning scenery, but not a whole lot to do unless you like walking.

dozle

I just spent a lovely, romantic weekend with my girlfriend in Wales. It was gorgeous, great little B&B on the top of a hill, beautiful view, lots of nice restaurants and bars (wonderful food), and easy to hop on a boat to Ireland in a couple of hours too.

liese

Oxford's lovely. I live here, so I take it for granted too much of the time, but if I didn't live here it's exactly the sort of place I'd visit – gorgeous buildings, museums and galleries, lots of pretty riverside outdoorness (including right in the city centre – try walking around Magdalen Deer Park and trying to get your head around the fact that you're bang in the middle of the city), stacks of great pubs and restaurants, and lots of nice countryside within 30–60 minutes' drive (the Vale of the White Horse to the south, and the Cotswolds to the west, in particular).

ej

Durham's got history – castle and cathedral. It's a city but it's not big. Bath is nice and you can often get nice hotels via Lastminute, it's got museums, history, galleries, shopping and some lovely restaurants.

k425

Pendle is a beautiful place – driving through it was like being immersed in The Hobbit – wonderful little streams completely covered by trees, and stunning escarpments and hills.

am

I have just remembered going to Rye for a friend's wedding, and how lovely it was. Have a look here: http://www.rye.org.uk/about_rye.htm

nb

Personally, I love Whitby – and there are plenty of B&Bs and good pubs for dinner.

gemma

FOOD INTOLER- ANCE AND EATING OUT

On the advice of my consultant I have cut dairy and wheat out of my diet (well, all but a few small lapses) over the last couple of months, and will be seeing a dietician shortly and doing an exclusion diet, after which I may have to avoid some other foods. I can't, or shouldn't, eat fatty foods (no gallbladder) and I lean towards being vegetarian, although I do eat fish.

Does anybody know of any good restaurants that cater for people with special eating requirements? Anywhere in the UK would be of interest, or even abroad.

land_girl

The Rainbow Vegetarian restaurant in Cambridge is very good – there are quite a few vegan things, and quite a few wheat-free things and a considerable overlap between them.

Indian restaurants are generally good as Indian cooking tends to be naturally dairy and wheat free, and there's normally a good vegetarian selection.

the_alchemist

Indian is generally difficult as even biryanis can have yoghurt in their marinades. Most sauces have dairy of some description (even if only ghee).

myf

Recently discovered that Cauldron Black Bean burgers have no wheat – don't know about dairy though.

gemma

Slug and Lettuce pubs are excellent: they point out all gluten-free stuff on the menu; my best friend is a coeliac who doesn't eat dairy, and I'm veggie, and it's a sure bet that we can always find something without having to traipse to the bar every few minutes to ask if something is gluten/meat/dairy free. We've never had any problems there, compared to rude waiters and bar staff refusing to ring the kitchen to ask. Wetherspoons also can get you a printed list of the dietary specs of all their food and are quite helpful. Not too great for a meal-out, but worth it if you're peckish and fancy a drink at the same time.

If you are ever in Nottingham city centre, the Alley Café bar is all veggie, and I think it's pretty good for other dietary requirements. I haven't tried it yet but Squeak is all veggie, and a proper restaurant. I've found veggie restaurants in general much better for actually knowing what goes into their food, and it's often low fat and healthier.

Also V1 is great for lunches: they're really good for accommodating meals to exclude dairy and wheat. And my final Nottingham recommendation is the Veggie Pot Indian.

skiescolliding

I have a wheat allergy, and I find Edinburgh fantastic for places which make their own food and can tell you EXACTLY what is in it, what it was prepared near, etc. There's lots of places that will accommodate you as much as possible. Takeaways are great too – Ricebox is really good, and even read labels of their non-homemade stuff to me over the phone! Original Khushis (Indian obviously) are great to eat out at. Also, importantly, there's a great veggie baked-tattie shop in town, so I can actually grab fast food that's healthy and won't leave me in agony for days!

batswing

It might also be worth checking out Bann's in Edinburgh, which is an excellent veggie restaurant. They are generally very helpful, and most of their menu is vegan or convertible to vegan. I imagine they'd be helpful with suggestions on the wheat side, too. And their puddings are fantastic!

Henderson's would also meet the bill but I personally find their veggie food a bit too 1970s worthy, but it's good if you like that kind of thing.

Bonsai in Newington is a good lower-priced Japanese, and Yumi is meant to be very good high-end Japanese. Ichiban in Glasgow is also nice if you end up there.

lisa g

In Manchester, Eighth Day on Oxford Road is a vegetarian restaurant with vegan and gluten-free options. Also, Bear Wholefoods in Todmorden.

k425

The Grain Shop on Portobello Road is lovely – you can't eat in, but a couple of doors down there's a nice bar you can eat the food in if you buy a drink. Govindas in Soho is quite nice. Wild Cherry Café in East London. And just to say that Bonsai in Edinburgh is one of my favourite restaurants. Damn, now I want sushi...

liese

El Piano in York does veggie and vegan food, and has gluten-free options too.

jj

In Ireland, western Ireland has a lot of coeliacs so a lot of restaurants actually understand gluten intolerance and either have it marked on the menu or will know! I love it because I'm borderline gluten intolerant!

wyvernfriend

Veggie/vegan places in central London:

- Neal's Yard Deli, Covent Garden
- Woodlands, off Marylebone High St
- Diwanas, Drummond St, nr Euston
- Food For Thought, Neal St., Covent Garden.

genie22

GETTING AWAY FROM IT ALL...

I'm planning to go on a chill out/retreat/health spa-type break, but having never done this before I've no idea where to start. I've had a look on the web for health spas and so on, but the obvious places seem to be very, very expensive. I appreciate that I will have to splash out a bit, but I don't want it to be so expensive that it defeats the object of the exercise – i.e. destress and have as many days as possible away from work/central London/general life. I've been through a period of high tension recently, and it's made me more anxious than I want to be... also, I'm getting bad back pain which isn't usually a problem.

Any thoughts? It doesn't have to be a health spa per se, but that's the closest I can think of that would do the trick. I want to go somewhere – either with a friend or alone, not decided yet – where I can just get away from it all for a bit, preferably with some health-promoting activities (yoga, swimming etc.) thrown in. I am not looking for beauty treatments or anything that means having particularly to talk to others all day – the plan is to escape from that!

starmix

Would you be willing to go abroad? I had the most wonderful life-affirming week at the end of September at http://www.hoho.co.uk/, and you can fly for about £100 if you're lucky. It was fabulous there – totally chilled. Yoga first thing in the morning by the pool, followed by a delicious fresh breakfast. Then there's treatments there if you want them, but if not there's a gorgeous pool, and the island has some incredibly beautiful places to go and see. Check this out http://www.lanzarote.com/LugJameos-in.html and it's SO much more beautiful in real life!

lm

You might laugh but I went to Center Parcs... they had a spa there and it was lubbly and really cheap. You can go for JUST spa breaks.

emma-leigh owen

If you just want a day out of it then try The Sanctuary in Covent Garden. I've heard some very good things and I use The Sanctuary bath stuff that you can buy in Boots. Lastminute.com do some good deals on spa breaks and about £100 can buy you an 8-hour day which includes breakfast, some alcohol, use of the pools, jacuzzi, saunas, steams rooms, relaxing lounges and an almost hour-long treatment of your choice (from a list). Oh and it's ladies only.

silvernik

DEBT AND USING PAYPLAN

Not had any personal experience, but Payplan are listed on the BBC watchdog Debt link with organisations like the CCCS and CAB which I've had very positive experiences with: http://www.bbc.co.uk/watchdog/links/finance/.

wp

Having just dealt with my own debt problems, I can honestly say that going to CAB and following their advice is a whole lot cheaper and better than using companies that may charge for their services – I don't know anything about Payplan, but if it is a company not a charity they must be making profit from you somewhere, right?

I sat down, worked out pro rata payments and did a budget (of doom), wrote to all my creditors and told them I was making an offer of payment of that amount, which they could see was pro rata. They all accepted, all letters and grim stuff went away, and I can eat once more! http://www.adviceguide.org.uk/index/life/debt/help_with_debt.htm

littlebluefish

Payplan are fine, they're paid for by a consortium of financial institutions so don't charge the people who use them a penny for their services. Also have a look at the CCCS and CAB.

The place I found most helpful of all when I was getting out of debt was the Dealing With Debt discussion board on Motley Fool – www.fool.co.uk. They're an amazingly friendly and helpful bunch of people, everything is anonymous, and if you post a statement of affairs on the board you'll get a load of advice on how to sort things out.

cazmanian minx

Payplan are fab and I've been with them for a year now! There are absolutely no fees and every penny you pay them goes straight to your creditors, and they also don't use your payments to negotiate interest rates.

I started off writing to my creditors with a budget and proposed payment plan, but they basically told me to sod off, so I went to Payplan and they asked me to fill in a budget sheet for them. They check it against the maximum allowed figures for each thing (like the government say you only need X amount for food and stuff) and adjust it as necessary. Originally I was doing a lot of travelling for work, so the amount I was spending on petrol was more than the allowed; they were great and just increased the things I wasn't on my maximum allowance for to make up the difference.

The best thing I've found is just not having to deal with creditors myself – they've negotiated it all, I pay them X amount a month and they split it up and pay it to everyone else.

oblivious

EATING CHOC‐ OLATE

Chocolate contains copper – very small amounts – but copper is lost during menstruation, and can help ease cramps.

caturah

Make it Fairtrade chocolate and you're doing Good In The World, as well!

la bias

What is all this obsession with chocolate? If I never ate another piece I would not miss it. When I was single, months, possibly years might go by without me ever buying any. Then the instant a bloke moves in, chocolate appears in the fridge, to be consumed in vast quantities by the male person. Real distress can occur when the chocolate runs out. (Again, from the bloke not me.)

In my experience, chocolate is a man thing. They get moody without regular doses. It must be their hormones. (I don't dislike chocolate, I'll eat it if it's there, but it never occurs to me to buy it myself as I never crave it. It's possible I could be some kind of alien tho'.)

md

The chemicals in chocolate (theobromine I think) do roughly the same thing to roughly the same bits of the brain as marijuana and the female orgasm. Plus, because it melts at below body temperature (and therefore melts on your tongue) it's a very sensuous food. Mainly, though, I just really like it.

sushidog

Theobromine also stops you coughing, according to some recent research!

sushidog

CHOCOLATE CRAVINGS

Is there anything I can take to stop my chocolate cravings?

exploitedfairy

I find drinking Yogi Tea Choco Aztec spice tea really helps – you can get it in health food shops and it's very chocolatey without being the real thing.

zoefruitcake

Lindt do an 85% bar that's very intense – like cocoa powder almost. I'd be surprised if anyone could eat much of that.

antigone76

I used to have a bad chocolate addiction and kicked it mostly with willpower I suppose. I stopped buying chocolate, which of course meant there was none in my flat; instead, I'd buy fruit and should I get a chocolate craving, I'd eat that instead. I used to buy Mars bars and stuff every morning on my way to work, so instead I'd take some of the fruit from the flat with me and not walk past the shops.

sara

Drinking lemon juice in water makes sweet things taste extra extra sweet. It's quite good for putting you off. I have a mug of hot water with the juice of half a fresh lemon in it every morning – really refreshing

tooth_fairy

Hypnotherapy – http://www.hypnosisdownloads.-com/downloads/health/chocolate-addiction.html – one of their tapes stopped me biting my nails.

gg

Bioforce make an extract of Jerusalem artichoke called 'Helix Slim' – it basically works if I recall correctly by raising your blood sugar levels slightly with good stuff instead of sugar, and it makes you less snacky, and curbs hunger until you're actually hungry. I've found it really helpful to avoid mid/late afternoon snack pangs, especially since they're as much a product of boredom with work as actual hunger. Definitely worth trying. It came with a big leaflet that told me all about how it works and what it does, so you don't have to reply on my dodgy memory – but I'd definitely recommend giving it a go. It's buyable at most health food-type places – anywhere that stocks the Bioforce range, really.

rillaith

Get some chromium GTF (glucose tolerance formula) while you're there too. It helps stabilise blood sugar, and at the same time generally knocks out cravings for sweet things.

sol

WANT CHOCOLATE?

Fairtrade, vegan, wheat free, diabetic... This site has an awful lot of it! http://www.alotofchocolate.co.uk/. They even do multisave on Green and Blacks, plus they do the dark Fairtrade Divine chocolate that only has 14 g carbs per 100 g, as opposed to the 45 g+ of other dark chocolates. Yay!

cookwitch

If you are a chocolate lover I recommend this page: http://www.hotelchocolat.co.uk/cx1/. For a small fortune (but worth it), they will send you a monthly box of chocolates. Now I have been known in the past to eat vast quantities of the stuff, but was unable to eat more than two of these chocs at one sitting, thanks to the flavour.

littlebluefish

Chocolate Trading Company is very good too.

cookwitch

ADVICE ON GIVING PRESENTATIONS AT JOB INTERVIEWS

- Stick to your time – practise and keep it to the specified time, that's all they'll have allowed in the schedule and they might stop you in full flow – plus it looks like you can't follow instructions.
- Professional-looking slides are worth the time and effort you spend doing them.

- Don't just read out what you've written – it makes you look wooden: paraphrase, make the same point in different words.
- Stick firmly to the point.

gg

The best advice I have for any sort of presentation is to start and end with a question to them. The starting question wakes them up a bit and gets them engaged, and the finishing question leaves them wanting to think about it more/talk to you more/generally be interested in you.

vicky l

It does depend on the role:

- Stick to time.
- Demonstrate how you fit the role.
- Make an effort to look outside the box. Demonstrate that you have spent time on this and thought about ways you could make a positive and lasting contribution.
- Professional slides are a good idea.
- Make sure you always have three items – dah dah and dah – because everyone feels lost with just two.

clare s

Practise. Lots. In front of the mirror, to your cat/mum/ the postman. Use notes on cards. Single word pointers about the item you want to mention. Know your stuff. Don't attempt to bluff because you will not be as clear as on those points where you know all the detail.

am

Basically, I think of it as a way of showing them that you've really thought about what the job entails and how you would envisage yourself doing it. When I had to do one, I talked about the types of information that prospective students would want, and why it benefited us to provide them with that information, and the different ways of disseminating information. I also used an OHP, because, um, it's kind of fun. And I do find OHP or Powerpoint presentations much easier to understand, when you've got bullet points to look at and remember while the person is talking.

la bias

STARTING YOUR OWN BUSINESS

Top things to remember are that you'll need to register with HMRC as self-employed, even if you're still employed, and you'll get sent tax returns.

Best thing to do would be to find your local Small Business Team in the tax office, and get them to point you at their free courses on being self-employed and running a business. It's also worth finding your local Business Link and talking to their business advisors.

kjaneway

As regards other advice, I'm sure you already know this, but MAKE A BUDGET! Go out and research the figures properly. Do market research, see what people want. No matter how fantastic the product is, there is no point making it if people don't have a need for it. Try and identify any gaps in the market.

hazyjayne

WRITING A COVERING LETTER

For the covering letter, have a look at the job description in the advert or any information they sent you, and try to think about how you fit the description. For example, can you demonstrate that you're enthusiastic about the subject area? Talking about studying for your A level might be good here, perhaps saying 'I was particularly interested in blah blah blah and enjoyed learning about thingamabob', picking out one or two of your favourite areas. For the 'strict deadlines' bit, you could mention that A level study includes an element of continuous assessment/coursework, which has required you to complete X number of dissertations, essays, portfolios, exercises or whatever, to a high standard and with a tight (non-negotiable) deadline.

Be specific where possible: saying 'I like numbers and stuff' doesn't sound very impressive, whereas 'I have a keen interest in mathematics and accounting, and have chosen to study them for my A level exams as well as being an active member of the Maths club for three years' is much better.

Be truthful though: if you make stuff up you're likely to get caught out, as they may ask you about it in the interview, or ask for proof!

sushidog

- Dear Sir/Madam > Yours faithfully
- Dear Name > Yours sincerely.
- This was drummed into us at school.
- Keep your covering letter short and to the point (no more than a page, including addresses).
- Mention something that you think makes you suited to the job (one sentence only). If the something is a qualification you have, say 'as you will see from my curriculum vitae (enclosed)...'.
- Make sure both letter and CV are properly spelled and punctuated, and conform to standard English grammar (typos or bad grammar create a disproportionately bad impression).
- If your CV is photocopied, make sure it's a crisp, clean copy. And don't forget to sign your letter (assuming you're not applying by e-mail).
- If you're not used to writing business letters, a quick trip to your local library is a good idea; somewhere in the 800s part of the non-fiction section (assuming your library uses the Dewey Decimal system) you will find books on how to write all kinds of business letters, including job applications.

k425

If at all possible, try to find out the name of the person you're sending your application to (it is perfectly acceptable to ring the company and ask for the name of the HR manager). It does create a good impression if your letter is addressed to the person responsible rather than a 'Sir/Madam' – shows that you've had the initiative to find out.

dorian

The CL is for you to really sell yourself, your CV tells them factually what you've done – this is the 'me' bit (er, for you, obviously). Tell them why you're interested in that job, what makes you stand out from the rest of the applicants – basically, why they should interview *you*.

Go through the job/person spec and pick out the key phrases and rework them to show you have experience of them. 'Team worker' – I was captain of the football team or whathaveyou if you have no 'actual' work experience.

*_mardybum_*

LIVING UP TO THE MAGAZINES

I was thinking about all the things I'm told to do whenever I read a magazine or newspaper or anything that gives advice on lifestyle. This is my list so far of what they want you to do:

- Spend several hours a day on make-up, grooming, clothes, hair, nails.
- Shop at local farmers' markets, greengrocers, butchers etc. instead of going to the supermarket.
- Don't drive anywhere, recycle, don't flush too much, don't fly.
- Don't use a computer too much.
- Don't watch TV.
- Do aerobics, yoga, martial arts, dance classes, running, swimming.
- Make healthy meals from scratch every day.
- Have mad passionate, yet safe, sex every night, but only with someone you're in love with and ideally are married to.
- Breastfeed, use terry nappies, learn baby massage, feed your children sprouts, educate them, play with them, leave them alone, protect them, punish them, don't punish them, run to them when they cry, ignore them when they cry, buy them toys, don't buy them toys, homeschool them, send them to public school, send them to

comprehensive school, send them to single-sex schools, send them to mixed-sex schools, teach them languages and music and drawing and sports. but don't make them feel pressured... this one's practically endless.

- Don't eat dairy, meat, chocolate, non-organic produce, anything with E numbers in, anything not grown in front of your eyes on a farm...
- Don't drink alcohol, milk, fruit juice, squash, tap water, mineral water, tea or coffee.
- Relax, stay alert, destress, achieve career success, stay at home with your children, work full-time.
- Stay single, get married, live with a partner, don't live with a partner, stay together, break up, find your one true love, sleep around, be a serial monogamist.
- Be thin, but not too thin.

Many of the above are good things to do – it's just that it's not actually possible to do more than a fraction of them, and everyone will disagree on which fraction.

What have I left out?

yh

Don't breathe – it take too much time and will prevent you doing all those things!

aellia

Have sophisticated dinner parties with like-minded stay-at-home mums and their understanding husbands.

sarah malaise

Don't go on diets, because they are bad for you and undermine your self-esteem, but do go on diets because you're a disgusting fat blob.

Have an immaculate home with endless clean clothes and ironed tablecloths, but for God's sake don't be all anally retentive about boring old housework!

anwen

There's probably a little bit of truth in all of them, but in order to make a good article they have to say 'Hey! Listen to this! This is true and interesting!' rather than 'Hmmm, well, there's this, and there's this, and this isn't really conclusive, but yada yada yada.' So 'RED WINE PREVENTS CANCER' and 'ALCOHOL KILLS BRAIN CELLS' make better headlines than 'A glass of red wine every now and then won't do you any harm, and may even be beneficial, and has probably been proved to slightly reduce the incidence of cancer in a non-zero percentage of rats, but it does kill brain cells, but they die all the time anyway, but hell, you know that if you drink too much you will be ill, so, y'know, be sensible, okay?'

The truth is probably out there somewhere, but personally I wouldn't be looking for it in lifestyle articles.

janet mcknight

Pah. Fie on magazines and newspapers and all that jazz. I do what I do because it's how I do it. Everyone else can just bugger off.

cookwitch

- Cleanse, tone and moisturise daily.
- Wax, pluck and shave everything.
- Have career, but don't forget to catch a man.
- Spend most of disposable income on hair, fashion and make-up.
- Keep man by learning sex tips from magazines.
- Get man to commit to you by using tips from magazines.
- Juggle career, babies, and keeping man happy in bed, without ever smudging make-up.

dozle

HOW TO GET ORGANISED...

I have so many things to do (obligatory things, things I want to do and things I enjoy doing) and yet I am a talented procrastinator (evidenced by the fact that I'm writing this rather than doing the things I should do/want to do). So, how exactly does one become an organised person? I start with so many good ideas and good intentions and then it all goes wrong – how do I make it work?

sera_squeak

Lists. For example, with my college work I have a list for the next two weeks of all my classes, what day they are, and what needs to be done. Then I can see how much work needs to be done for when, and can see what will take longer and therefore should be done sooner. Then I cross off what's been done.

I also recommend a tidy space – my desk is always clear before I start studying, then I can find everything immediately and don't faff around looking for things.

Take breaks in whatever you are doing – perhaps alternate between the stuff you don't want to do and the fun stuff, so that by the end of the day you've achieved two things but it's not been too unpleasant.

I'm afraid I think it's about discipline (not the fun sort) and planning and just accepting that you have to get on with things, but then you can also appreciate that when you've done the crappy tasks you can relax and know they are finished, and do something fun.

kauket

I found the book *Getting Things Done* by David Allen really useful in getting myself a bit more organised. He's very into to-do lists, but the important part is that your list should actually include on it The Next Physical Thing I Should Do On This Project, rather than just 'do X', where X is a large thing with lots of steps to be taken. Gives you a far better idea of what you're doing.

The other things I regularly use for motivation are either to use a timer (set it for 15 minutes, do 15 minutes of X, then I'm allowed to play on LJ/knit/ whatever for 15 minutes), or similarly, put a CD on and do X (or tackle stuff on my work to-do list, or whatever) until the end of the CD.

jk

I found Flylady useful in terms of taking some of the good bits (e.g. doing stuff for 15 minutes, not getting hung up on perfection, doing something rather than nothing as every little bit helps, and timetabling in stuff to do for yourself), and ignoring the irritating bits. I have bullied Himself into making the bed when he gets out of it (he works from home and therefore gets up a couple of hours after me), as it does make me feel better when it's made, even badly. Similarly, I've found that spending 5 or 10 minutes picking things up on a regular basis makes a massive difference to how the place looks, and I really prefer it that way – far less stressful.

My partner and I now have a fortnightly list of chores divided between us (swap over each fortnight), and I can get mine done a bit at a time over the fortnight, which I like.

jk

To do lists, schedules, self-imposed deadlines.

It may sound obvious, but you need to have a diary with everything pencilled in, and consult it so you're always aware of timeframes.

It never ceases to amaze me that many people, for example, while well aware that task A needs doing, have no idea of when it needs finishing. So you say to them, you only have two days to get task A done and they say, 'what! I thought it was weeks away.' Understandably, this results in delays, rushed work or stuff not getting done at all.

Another tip: if you have a massive scary task that just seems too big and impossible to tackle at all, break it down into a list of tiny tasks to cross off one by one as you do them. You stop being paralysed by a task being too big and terrifying, and get on with nibbling away at small bits of it.

md

The 'next actions' idea is one of the best things about GTD. Basically, he divides things into 'projects' (anything that requires more than one action to finish) and 'actions'. A lot of people will have on their to-do list things like (from my own recent list at work) 'Sort out new backup system', 'Revamp local webpages', 'Prepare dead toner cartridges for recycling'. The last one of those isn't so bad, but the other two are entirely useless to have on a list. Every time you look at them you think 'Oh God how can I start on that, what should I do next' and then you get all panicky and don't do anything.

So for those examples, the next actual Thing I Need To Do on each:

- Sort out new backup system:

    □ work out how much storage space we actually need (after that, FWIW, it has so far gone like this:
    □ ask for suggestions from relevant email list
    □ get quotes from suppliers for different systems/sizes
    □ write up quotes
    □ talk to head of dept to confirm purchases
    □ get quotes for tape media
    □ put purchase order through
    □ every time I do an action, I cross that off and add the Next Thing To Do to the list.

- Revamp local webpages:

□ read through them and make notes on what
    needs to change
□ draft new structure

- and then I did a section at a time.

He also talks about dealing with 'pending' things
and 'possible' things, and so on. I'd strongly recommend reading GTD if this sounds like it would be
useful! Although obviously I'm not necessarily
recommending following it to the letter (I certainly
don't) – I'm a big fan of adapting systems to your own
needs, taking useful bits and leaving the rest etc.

jk

NOT A MORNING PERSON

**That's what I am. I've always been really crap in
the mornings. I wake up and I don't feel I can
get out of bed, I'm tired up until lunchtime most
days.**

**I don't really go to bed all that late. Usually 11
at the latest, sometimes 9.30 or 10. But, I can't
get to sleep right away. I wish I could just drop
right off but I don't – I lie there and think about
stuff – stuff that happened in the past, things that
might happen in the future, stuff people said,**

things I've read about blah blah blah. I just go
over and over things in my mind. And I dream a
lot, some of the dreams are really intense.

So I'm wondering if this is why I'm always
tired in the mornings? 'Cos my mind isn't rested
when I go to bed? Maybe my brain isn't rested
'cos I think too much about stuff at night, and
perhaps I'm tossing and turning with all this
dreaming I do?

Any suggestions?

luthiea

Try Kalms, and reading something funny and light
before bed, to give you something better to think
about, and the Kalms might help you have calmer
sleep once you do drop off.

Good sleep is a habit. It can be learned, apparently,
unless you have Other Issues. Good luck.

ailbhe

Or a book that you know really well and doesn't
require much mental effort. I confine my bedtime
reading to 'fluff' that I've read several times before –
it's much easier to put down a book when it's light-
weight and I know what's going to happen. Otherwise, I too read till 3 am to see what happens next!
(And I stick to very light literature because anything
that requires concentration is going to make me more
awake, rather than relaxing me.)

Old childhood favourites are very good bedtime
reading, I find.

dorian

Related to the story thing, my way to stop thoughts just whirling round and round is to put music that I don't know all that well on, and concentrate on listening to the lyrics, so that my mind can't do anything else.

pickwick

I doubt that the dreaming is causing you to sleep badly; rather, it'll be the other way round. We all dream for a significant portion of each night (if we don't, we tend to go mad fairly quickly!), but we only remember dreams if we wake up quite soon after having them, because we don't form memories while asleep.

It sounds as though perhaps you need some 'winding down' time before bed, to help you to sleep better. A warm milk drink would be a good idea (there are naturally occurring chemicals in warmed milk that help to combat stress), as would a warm bath before bedtime. Try not to eat within two hours of bedtime, and while it would be good to do some physical exercise during the day, again this shouldn't be within two hours of bed.

If you're worrying about particular things when you go to bed, it might be worth spending half an hour in the evening concentrating on those things, deciding what you can do about them, and making a 'to-do' list for the next day. When you've done that, you can give yourself permission to stop thinking about them. Then go to bed, and try some deep breathing exercises (breathing in slowly to the count of five, then breathing out slowly to a count of six, thinking 'relax' or 'peaceful' or 'sleep' on each breath). If other thoughts intrude, try to push them out of your mind, just thinking to yourself 'I shall think about that tomorrow, but not now', and try to clear your mind, or think of something very relaxing and calm; visualise, in detail, a beautiful desert island, or a cosy room with a fireplace, or whatever works for you. It sounds trite, but it can be very effective!

sushidog

Another relaxation thing that can be helpful is to start at your toes and tense and relax every muscle in your body, slowly working upwards. If you're still awake when you get to the top, breath slowly and deeply (as above) and use the calm visualisation stuff sushidog mentions. I find this works pretty effectively most of the time.

jk

I find going to sleep really hard – the parliament program on Radio 4 works like a dream. The droning voices work perfectly, and I wake up with all sorts of interesting political knowledge with which to impress friends!

littlebluefish

HOUSING LAW ADVICE

The Leasehold Advisory Service provides free advice on the law affecting residential long leasehold property and commonhold: http://www.lease-advice.org/newintro.htm.

suzylou

DATA RECOV-ERY

My laptop fell over and died at the weekend, total hard disk crash, and of course I've not backed it up in far too long, and of course it has all my PhD research on it. Anyone know anyone who does data recovery at reasonable rates? The one quote I had so far was about £700!!!

suzylou

£700 is about what I would expect to pay, I'm afraid. I had to do this last month and paid £500 or so plus VAT.

renarde

My work laptop hard disk fell over in January 2005 and I used Fields Data Recovery. I would recommend them. Also you can send your disk to them and they'll investigate and give you a free (fixed) quote, as well as the price guides on their website.

westernind

Data recovery from a shagged hard drive is *Difficult*. There's a good reason why it's so expensive.

kjaneway

Vogon – my boss's hard disk died and they got stuff off it. The IT chap took it to them – but not cheap at all. When asked why, they were heard to say 'we find that customers review their backing-up policies after speaking to us...'

bee

PAINTING

When you're decorating a room, do the ceiling first and work down. Paint never runs uphill. As I wish my dad had told me at the time, rather than just watching politely.

kp

LINKWORD LANGUAGE COURSES

Linkword is a brilliant system; many years ago my parents had the Spanish Linkword book and I spent some time with it, and even now I can remember some of the words that I learned:

- Gato = Cat (imagine a cat eating a big gateau)

- Raton = Mouse (imagine a rat sitting on a mouse)
- Avispa = Wasp (imagine a wasp a-whispering in your ear)

It really is stunningly effective, because it isn't just about trying to remember something for the sake of remembering – it actually gives you a reason to remember. I'll stop rambling and just say: Highly Recommended.

morganalefay

AND
FINALLY...

Tea and bubble baths solve just about anything.

batswing

Acknowledgements

The editors would like to thank the following people for allowing their contributions to be used in this book:

mardybum, AB, Abi Silvester, AG, ailbhe, Ali Willis, ALT, AM, Amy Marie Mason, Angel Johnson, Anna Blight, Anna Brown, Anna R. Bradley, Annabel Crerar, AD, Antigone77, Anwen, April Middleton, Ara Maye, Becca Courtley, Becky Annison, Bee, boneist, Bonnie Gough, Brane, Bryony King, Caroline Cormack, Caroline Jones, CC, Ceiswyn, Claire Reay, Clare Spurway, Debbie Mac Rory, Deborah Crook, Deirdre Ruane, Desiring Cairo, DF, Donna McMahon, Dorian, Duckiemonster, Easterbunny, Ebee, EC, Eldelphia, Eleanor Blair, Eleanor Orebi Gann Elise Harris, Elizabeth Lovegrove, Emily, Emma-Leigh Owen, ES, Exploitedfairy, FA, Feath, FGC, Gemma Wright, Gill, Glassarmy, halluciphy, Hannah Elwick, Hazel Leivars, hazyjayne, Helen Dixon, HK, how_I_lie, HS, hyzenflay, Il-Maltija, Isobel, Jackie Joseph, Janet McKnight, Jeni Law, Jess Bennett, JK, Jo, JP, Judith Crunch, juggzy, Jules, Julie, JZ, Karen Martin, Kat Stevens, Kate Atkin-Wright, Kate B, Kate Sinclair, kauket/KK, kaz_pixie, Kelly White, KG, Kim Bond, kissycat1001, KP, ladyblaize, ladyynara, lahermite, land_girl, Lannie, laumiere, Laura, Laura Creaven, Laura Porter, Liese Lewyckyj, Lindsay Endell, Lisa Feinson, Lisa G, Lisa Wolf, littlebluefish, Livre d'Or, Liz Babb, Lizzie Reed, Lizzie Ward, Lizzy Muggeridge, lostprophet, lothie, Louisa J King, loulou, LP, Lucrezia Borgia, Lucy Kennedy, Luthiea, Maddie Telford, Madeleine, Mandy, Maria, Mary Macfarlane, meepettemu, Mendi, Michelle Thomson, misswilde, missyk9, mistytwiglet, MJ, MJF, MK, mmcpoland, mollydot, morganalefay, mtb0002, naath, Natalie Mott, Nicky Saunders, Nicola Blay, Nikki, Nina Blakesley, nita_01nita, nurse_liz, oblivious, MC, PB, Penny Little, pickwick, pipistrellus, princesswannabe, pumpkin, quorta, R.A-B, Rainbow, rainsinger, ramtops, Rebecca McAllister, red_panda_bear, renarde, rmc29, rougeforever, Sadie Slater, Sajini Wijetilleka, Sally Gurney, Sally Humphrys, Samantha Keighley, Sara, Sarah Malaise, schmoomom, SD, sea_of_flame, secretrebel, Seonaid Ashford, Sera Fisher, seren, sesquipedality, shermarama, shewho, Shira Sandler Becket, Shreena, silja, Silke, silverclear, silverfiligree, silverixney, silvernik, siren, slemslempike, SOL, Sophie Mobbs, sue Houghton, suicideally, sushidog, suzylou, SW, syleth, T, tamaranth, Tania Qoura, Tania Reilly, TB, TD, TI, teqkiller, terriem, Tess Flynn, TG, the_alchemist, TM, TT, tvor, Vampwillow, VF, VGHarris, Vicky Larmour, vinaigrettegirl, westernind, wey, WP, wyvernfriend, yanata, zoefruitcake.

Thanks to genie22 for looking through the Health chapter, and thanks to the Loos members who helped to trawl the archives looking for material.

Katy is very grateful to Simon, Marcus, George and a wide variety of her friends for their help and support. She would like to thank her two-year-old daughter Holly, but she's not going to, since Holly's help consisted of continually tugging on her arm and saying 'Mummy, stop doing that and play with me'. Any errors in the book should therefore be blamed on Holly.

Natasha would like to thank her husband Joe Mugford for his help and for doing a lot more housework than her. She appreciates her mother, Anne Morabito, and friends Jody Thompson and Catherine Mellor, who were there when she got the fear. She is grateful to her colleagues Claire Telford and Rowan O'Sullivan, who lent their support and told her to 'calm down' a lot.

Index